Shanghai Lalas

Queer Asia

The Queer Asia book series opens a space for monographs and anthologies in all disciplines focused on non-normative sexuality and gender cultures, identities and practices in Asia. Queer Studies and Queer Theory originated in and remain dominated by North American and European academic circles, and existing publishing has followed these tendencies. However, growing numbers of scholars inside and beyond Asia are producing work that challenges and corrects this imbalance. The Queer Asia book series—first of its kind in publishing—provides a valuable opportunity for developing and sustaining these initiatives.

Recent titles in the series

As Normal as Possible: Negotiating Sexuality and Gender in Mainland China and Hong Kong
Edited by Yau Ching

Queer Bangkok: 21st Century Markets, Media, and Rights
Edited by Peter A. Jackson

Falling into the Lesbi World: Desire and Difference in Indonesia
Evelyn Blackwood

Queer Politics and Sexual Modernity in Taiwan
Hans Tao-Ming Huang

Conditional Spaces: Hong Kong Lesbian Desires and Everyday Life
Denise Tse-Shang Tang

Contact Moments: The Politics of Intercultural Desire in Japanese Male-Queer Cultures
Katsuhiko Suganuma

Queer Singapore: Illiberal Citizenship and Mediated Cultures
Edited by Audrey Yue and Jun Zubillaga-Low

Shanghai Lalas

Female *Tongzhi* Communities and Politics in Urban China

Lucetta Yip Lo Kam

香港大學出版社
HONG KONG UNIVERSITY PRESS

Hong Kong University Press
The University of Hong Kong
Pokfulam Road
Hong Kong
www.hkupress.org

ISBN 978-988-8139-45-3 *(Hardback)*
ISBN 978-988-8139-46-0 *(Paperback)*

British Library Cataloguing-in-Publication Data
A catalogue record for this book is available from the British Library.

Cover photo: "Karaoke" by Shitou, 2006.

10 9 8 7 6 5 4 3 2 1

Printed and bound by Goodrich Int'l Printing Co., Ltd. in Hong Kong, China

For *lalas* in China

Contents

Acknowledgements

This book is about and for the *lala* communities in China and Shanghai in particular. I am very grateful to all who have shared the most intimate details of their lives with me. I would like to thank Laoda for her trust and for introducing me to the local *tongzhi* communities, and all *lala* comrades in China for allowing me to stand with them to fight all those battles against social prejudices and for tolerating my presence as a cultural outsider. (I am grateful to them too for helping me improve my *putonghua*). A big thank-you goes to the Chinese *Lala* Alliance (CLA) (華人拉拉聯盟) for enriching my knowledge of the LBT communities across the country. My work experience with the CLA allowed me to understand the diversities in LGBTQ movements among different Chinese societies.

This book was completed in the years when I underwent many life challenges. I thank my friends for supporting me through all those ups and downs. I am very grateful to the following friends (in alphabetical order of surname): Eunice Au, Anita Chan, Clarice Cheung, Eleanor Cheung, Chen Yi-chien, Joyce Chiu, Joseph Cho (Siu Cho), Joey Chung, Thomas Gamble, Nguyễn Tân Hoàng, Dredge Kang, Mary Ann King (Gum Gum), Ashley Ko, Franco Lai, Vice Selina Lam, Lily Lau, Karen Lee, Helen Leung, Joanne Leung, Pik Ki Leung, Yvonne Leung, Sophie Lin, Anson Mak, Fran Martin, Tan Ee Lyn, June Tang, Grace To, Day Wong, Cecily Yam, Audrey Yue, Ellen Yuen, and my dear *lala* friends in China.

My sincere gratitude goes to my doctoral thesis supervisors, Eric Ma and Yip Hon-ming. They provided intellectual and emotional support throughout my graduate studies. I would also like to thank the Gender Studies Programme at the Chinese University of Hong Kong. The programme funded my graduate studies and most part of this research. I especially thank Po-king Choi (Boyee) for her care, support and spiritual enlightenment. I was most fortunate to have a group of fabulous fellow classmates, who created a supportive and inspiring environment for me to conduct my study.

In developing my doctoral thesis into a book, I am grateful for the comments and encouragement of John Nguyet Erni, Anthony Fung, Gayatri Gopinath, Saori Kamano, Diana Khor, Travis Kong, Helen Leung, Fran Martin, Yau Ching, Audrey Yue, and the two anonymous reviewers of this book's draft manuscript. I also thank the editors of the Queer Asia book series and Hong Kong University Press for publishing this book.

Finally, I thank my family—Freda Cho, Jo Kam and Hillman Wong—for their love and for always being there for me.

Introduction: Reconnecting Selves and Communities

On 4 June 2005, I was invited to a private party at a karaoke lounge in downtown Shanghai. I was told it was a surprise proposal party between two women. I followed my new *lala*[1] friends to a splendidly decorated karaoke complex and entered one of the small rooms. More than ten women were already waiting inside. I saw candles and rose petals on the table. Without knowing who these women were or what was going to happen, I joined them in lighting up the candles and arranging them into two hearts, one big and one small. Rose petals were sprinkled around the candles and a bouquet of flowers was at the ready. Cameras were placed on standby. Not long after we finished decorating, the couple arrived. The one to be proposed to was stopped outside the door. The woman who was to propose entered the room. Lights switched off. We all stood in a circle around the candlelit hearts, expectant. Then the door was opened, and the woman knelt down and held out the bouquet to her lover. Her lover was totally caught by surprise. Everyone erupted into cheers of joy. This happened on the first day of my ethnographic research in Shanghai.

As an ignorant newcomer who had just learnt the term "*lala*", I did not expect to join such an intimate party with a group of *lala* women whom I had known for just a few hours. The two lovers in the party were both in heterosexual marriages. Looking back, this party directed me to a few themes that later became major areas of investigation in my research. These themes included the development of local *lala* communities, the institution of heterosexual family and marriage, the emerging *tongzhi* family and marriage, and *lala* women's everyday strategies in coping with family, marriage and society.

Begun in 2005, this ongoing research project is an ethnographic study of *lala* women in Shanghai and one of the first participatory investigations of emerging *tongzhi* politics and communities in China. It is being carried out at a time when individuals are being connected to form *tongzhi* communities, and when new identities are being created by previously stigmatized sexual subjects for self-empowerment. "*Lala*" has become a collective identity for women with same-sex desires and other non-normative gender and sexual identifications. "*Tongzhi*", as a term originated in communist China and re-invented in Hong

Kong, has returned to its place of origin as an entirely rejuvenated public identity for a community of people who had for decades been denied visibility in society. These newly invented public identities for non-normative sexualities and genders have created new selves and subjectivities. New understandings of self lead to new aspirations of life which also introduce challenges to the existing norms of the heterosexual institution. The formation of *tongzhi* communities in post-reform China (after 1979) has highlighted the discrepancy between a self-assertive *tongzhi* subjecthood and the denial and rejection many *tongzhi* encounter in their families. This has led me to consider the changing forms of challenges faced by *lala* women in China. New discourses of subjectivity, new forms of intimacy and new ways of social networking have been made available by the *tongzhi* communities. New opportunities, together with new modes of regulation, are being presented in post-reform China. Given all these emergent resources and restrictions, in what ways are the lives of *lala* women different from those in the past? How would they deal with their newly adopted *tongzhi* identity and in particular, with the pressure to marry?

This book aims to look at the negotiation between the new life aspirations of *lala* identified women and the existing heterosexual requirements imposed on them. In particular, when family and marriage are frequently reported as the major causes of stress in their everyday life, how do they reconcile their newly acquired understanding of the self with forces of heterosexual conformity? I intend to address the following questions: What impact do ongoing public discourses on homosexuality and *tongzhi* have on the everyday existence of *lala* women? How do public discourses inform and regulate the construction of a new *tongzhi* subjectivity and politics in China? In particular, how would this new *tongzhi* subjectivity affect *lala* women's struggle against a culture that dismisses women's sexual autonomy and subjectivity? In other words, what kind of *tongzhi* politics will be generated under the current social context of post-reform China? To individual *lala* women, what is the impact of the emergence of *lala* communities to their everyday lives, especially their coping strategies with the institution of heterosexuality? How can emerging forms of *tongzhi* intimacy, such as cooperative marriage (*hezuohunyin* or *xingshihunyin*),[2] lead to a critical re-examination of the dominant rules of heteronormativity, and open up new imaginations of family and marriage? Most importantly, what kind of future can we imagine with all of the lived practices of intimacy and *tongzhi* activism in China?

Project *"Tongzhi"*

Among the numerous ongoing social changes in post-reform China, "*tongzhi*"— as a rejuvenated identity—is the focus of attention that is often viewed in close association with the transformation of China. It has been understood in the context of transnational LGBTQ movements and politics, and is often discussed in the context of the construction of new citizenship in post-reform China. As a newly introduced sexual subjectivity, "*tongzhi*" has emerged from a history of social and political stigmatization, and still remains a battlefield of discursive struggles among different actors in the public. Local *tongzhi* communities, the general public, experts, scholars, and the state are all eager to indoctrinate their own definitions of "*tongzhi*". The contents of "*tongzhi*" are yet to be filled up.

The year 2005 alone saw the formation of the first grassroots *lala* organization in Shanghai, the first meeting of female *tongzhi* groups from all over the country in Beijing and the birth of *les+* (www.lesplus.org), the first *lala* magazine in China. So much happened in a single year. The last decade has been an important formative period of the *tongzhi* community in China. The last five years, in particular, has witnessed a rapid development of local *lala* communities in different parts of China.

Communication technologies have played a vital role in connecting individuals and forming communities. When the Internet opened up to popular use in the late 1990s, discussions of homosexuality first appeared on forums with names understood only by insiders. Into the millennium, independent *lala* websites began to crop up. The three most popular *lala* websites for local women in Shanghai—*Aladao* (阿拉島), *Shenqiuxiaowu* (深秋小屋) and *Huakaidedifang* (花開的地方, also known as *Huakai*)—were all developed in the early 2000s. In 2005, *Huakai* had more than 40,000 registered members. The Internet also accelerated the interflow of *tongzhi* culture among Chinese societies. Due to linguistic, geographical and cultural affinities between the three societies, lesbian culture and activism in Hong Kong and Taiwan have always served as important reference points for *lala* women in China. With the organizing of regional activities, the interflow of information, texts and people intensified all the more. For instance, *Lala* Camp is a significant platform of cultural dialogue among lesbian communities in China, Hong Kong and Taiwan. It is an annual training camp held in China for Chinese-speaking lesbian organizers from China, Hong Kong, Macau, Taiwan and the overseas. Started in 2007, when organizers of local *lala* communities in participating regions gathered in a southern city in China, *Lala* Camp has since become an important breeding ground for *lala* organizing in China. It has also acted as an important discursive site for Chinese *tongzhi* politics.

To the general public, the latest popular use of "*tongzhi*" refers to "homosexual people". To the younger generation, the term has successfully departed from the older meaning of communist "comrades". More often, homosexual people are referred to as "*tongxinglian*" in public discussions. In mainland Chinese academia, "*tongxinglian*" is more widely used than "*tongzhi*".

Therefore, "*tongzhi*" is more often synonymous with "*tongxinglian*" in everyday usage. While there have been efforts in *tongzhi* communities to expand the term to include homosexual, bisexual, asexual, transgender and queer identified individuals, however public discussions still predominantly use the term "*tongxinglian*". The conflated use of the two terms is common.

Homosexuality, especially male homosexuality, has caught much public attention in recent years. In the economic reform era, in a context of changing attitudes towards sex and private life in China, public understanding of homosexuality was under constant reinterpretation and debate in academic studies, and by popular culture and everyday conversations. State-run bookstores sold books on homosexuality. Surveys on the social acceptance of homosexuality were conducted by state media.[3] Leading up to today, the growing amount of media coverage, the appearance of homosexual people on prime time television programmes, the heated debates on homosexuality on Internet forums, and the more recent popularity of "boy's love" comics (or BL comics) and gay stories on micro-blogs (*weibo*) among the younger generation demonstrate the curiosity of the general public about the previously silenced subject matter.

The new public interest in homosexuality has developed against a backdrop of changing social control in recent decades. Individual mobility, both geographical and social, had increased significantly during the reform period. Then, since the 1990s, increased geographical mobility of individuals has led to the emergence of urban *tongzhi* subcultures in many major cities in China. In addition, the opening up of the labour market has led to the weakening of direct state control through the *danwei*—the central job assignment system— over people's private lives.

On the ideological front, there has been a paradigmatic change in state control over homosexuality in China since the late 1990s. Two major changes have taken place at legal and medical establishments. Homosexuality was excluded from legal prosecution through the abolishment of "hooliganism" from Article 160 of the old Criminal Law in 1997, which was applied to male homosexual activities in the past. It was then further removed from the medical category of perverts by the Chinese Psychiatry Association in 2001. These two changes have been generally regarded as the decriminalization and depathologization of (male) homosexuality in China; however, legal, medical and other forms of state and social prohibition of homosexuality are still widely present. At the same time, social control of homosexuality has increasingly manifested through a rhetoric of public health and public security. Male homosexuality is particularly constructed by the state as a risk to public health and social stability. On the other hand, female homosexuality is marginalized in public discussion, and is rarely represented in mainstream media. This has generated two common observations made about the public discussion and representation of homosexuality in China: namely, an over-representation of views from a heterosexual position and a disproportionate amount of attention given to male homosexuality.

Public discussions and academic studies on homosexuality and *tongzhi* overwhelmingly presume a heterosexual position. The fact that the *tongzhi* is always "talked about" and constructed as the "other"—as raised by Harriet Evans regarding earlier studies done by Chinese scholars—gives rise to "the potential of misinterpretation and distortion" (Evans 1997, p. 209). As an improvement, first-person accounts of same-sex relationships have entered the public spotlight in recent years. But the risk of othering and stereotypical representations still persist, with moralistic, heteronormative values underlying the majority of public voices. As for the under-exposure of female homosexuality in public discussions and academic studies, the reasons are multifold. Li Yinhe and Wang Xiaobo (1992), Ruan Fangfu (1991), Zhang Beichuan (1994) and Lisa Rofel (1997) mention the difficulty of locating "homosexual women" in China. Since these research studies were mostly conducted in the 1990s, one possible explanation is that *lala* communities with greater visibility have developed only after those of gay men. Another explanation is a prevalent cultural dismissal of female sexuality. In terms of legal control, female homosexual practices are generally considered to be a much lesser threat to public security than male homosexual practices. Therefore, it is comparatively rare for women to be penalized for same-sex sexual activities, though in the 1980s there were still cases of women being detained for homosexual "sex crimes", as documented by Ruan (1991). The lenient treatment of female homosexuals by the authorities reflects a history of cultural dismissal of erotic activities between women. Being a subordinate group in the gender hierarchy, women's "abnormal" sexual behaviour is considered less threatening to the dominant social order. This cultural prejudice against female sexuality provides a less regulated and less punitive social space for women with same-sex desires and practices. However, it also contributes to the symbolic erasure of female homosexuality in public imagination, and directly affects the development of local *lala* communities. It especially affects the funding sources of local *lala* groups. *Tongzhi* activism in China has largely originated and been carried out through the discourse of AIDS prevention and public health. Sources of funding within and outside the country have always been offered to sexual health projects for the homosexual population. *Lala* women are usually excluded from obtaining resources that are assigned to sexual health projects. As a result, they are not only disadvantaged in securing resources but are also marginalized from gaining public attention. In most cases, they have to rely on the material resources of gay men to carry out their projects and to develop communities. The *"Tongxin* Female *Tongzhi* Hotlines"* and the more recent *"800 Lala* Hotline" in Shanghai are two typical examples of how *lala* women rely on gay resources to offer support services for their own communities.

Compulsory Marriage

On the private front, one recurring theme that emerged over the course of my interviews was the conflict between *lala* women's desire to have same-sex relationships and the familial expectation for them to get married. For married informants, the pressure was expressed in the conflict between a heterosexual marriage and an extra-marital same-sex relationship. As mentioned earlier, family and personal lives, strictly controlled and monitored by the *danwei* system and the community surveillance system before the reform era, have been largely released from direct state control during China's economic transformation into a market economy. There has been a gradual shift from collective interests to individual rights and choices in the domain of private life. Direct state control of private lives has shifted to a more intimate form of daily scrutiny conducted by one's immediate family and social networks. Family members, especially the seniors, act as inspectors of the private life of younger ones. For non-normative sexual subjects, the heterosexual family is usually the biggest source of stress in their daily lives. The heterosexual family and marriage are as important as various public forms of social control in contemporary China as major sources of heterosexual policing. The nature of their control over non-normative sexual subjects, for example, through the rhetoric of love and familial harmony, is yet to be fully examined.

The compulsory nature of marriage puts *lala* women at a disadvantaged position. *Lala* women are denied recognition as autonomous sexual subjects in Chinese culture. While both unmarried women and men are considered as immature persons or not as autonomous beings, unmarried women are further rejected as autonomous sexual subjects. Women's sexuality is not recognized under the cultural belief of a male-active/female-passive sexual model. The monogamous heterosexual marriage further naturalizes a woman's receptive role in sexual relations with a man. In such a culture where women's sexual inactivity is treated as the very foundation of gender relationships and hierarchies, it is tremendously difficult for non-heterosexual women to be recognized as active sexual subjects. One consequence is that it makes coming out a tricky and doubly difficult task for *lala* women. A *lala* woman has to come out not only as a homosexual subject, but also as foremost as a legitimate and autonomous sexual subject. Moreover, the stigma against unmarried or divorced women is still widely present even in cosmopolitan cities like Shanghai. Marriage is culturally understood as *the* rite of passage to adulthood. This belief particularly affects women's autonomy in opting for alternative living arrangements. Many native Shanghai women told me that the only way for them to move out of their parents' home would be to get married. Marriage is the only way for them to break away from parental control and be treated as autonomous individuals. For *lala* women married to heterosexual partners, divorce is not always a viable option. A divorce would involve families of both sides in a similar way as a marriage does, and consequently, a failed marriage would also be regarded as a failure to fulfil one's familial expectation. The compulsory nature of marriage, its role as the only endorsement of adulthood, and the conjugal union as the only recognized form of family form a persistent and primary source of stress for *tongzhi* in China. One primary focus of this book is to critically examine the pressures of marriage faced by *lala* women and their coping strategies in resisting heteronormative social demands.

Personal and Political Significance

This research is significant to me both personally and politically. I am a Shanghai native who migrated to Hong Kong at an early age. I am also an active member of the *tongzhi* community in Hong Kong, and who later became involved in *tongzhi* activism in China. This research allowed a number of (re)connections involving personal experiences, cultural and political identifications. It reconnected me with my birthplace and my fading memories of a happy childhood in Shanghai during the 1970s. It connected my participation within different *tongzhi* communities. It was through this research that I was able to engage myself in a dialogue between *tongzhi* communities in Hong Kong and China. I indeed found myself constantly cross-referencing experiences in both communities. The research created an intellectual space for me to contemplate *tongzhi* politics in both societies from a position other than an insider. The exercise of (re)connecting and disconnecting among multiple roles and perspectives enriched my understanding beyond the self and *tongzhi* communities. It allowed me to engage in an inner dialogue with my own positions on gender, sexuality, ethnicity, class, age and cultural identity. It also sharpened my insights into both societies. Hong Kong is politically a part of China, and is connected with the mainland geographically, culturally, economically and relationally through the people. However, doing ethnography in China, even as it was in a city where I spent my childhood and have extensive family ties, was still a cultural adventure into a *new* old world. I had to keep my eyes open to minute everyday norms such as rituals of interpersonal interaction, hierarchies of social relations, perceptions of personal boundaries, down to unspoken rules about avoiding bicycles while walking on the pavement. The learning of micro customs in daily life proved to be instructive in understanding the everyday challenges *tongzhi* face in China. In particular, as a woman who is not in a heterosexual marriage, I understood more how unmarried women are marginalized or sometimes even harassed in social situations because of their gender, age and marital status, and how people (especially those who are married) in their families, workplace or even on the streets pay a smothering concern to their personal lives and future life plans.

My personal engagement in this research became even more pronounced after I became involved in *tongzhi* activism in China. Shortly after I started my research, I introduced a local Hong Kong oral history project of "women loving women", in which I was a committee member, to the *lala* community in Shanghai.[4] They later launched their own project documenting *lala* women's life stories in Shanghai. It resulted in an internally circulated book entitled *Talking about Their Love: An Oral History of Women Who Love Women in Shanghai I (Tamen de ai zaishuo: Aishang nüren de nüren. Shanghai. Koushulishi I)* (2008) by Shanghai *Nvai* Lesbian Group, the first grassroots *lala* organization in Shanghai. I participated as a trainer for oral-history interview and, up until now, remain as a consultant to the project. Later, I became a committee member of the Chinese *Lala* Alliance (CLA), a cross-regional alliance of Chinese-speaking lesbian, bisexual and transgender women, and am still a member of its advisory board.

The dual roles of a researcher and an activist generate concerns over research ethics. In my case, it required my constant effort in managing my roles in different contexts. As a researcher, the *tongzhi* community was a "field" to be studied, documented and analysed. As an activist, it was a community that I personally identified with. Tensions resulted at times when I needed to choose either role; while at other times, the two roles were smoothly combined. More reflections on role management are presented in "Notes on Methodology" on p. 12.

Through engaging in *tongzhi* activism in China, I learnt about the diversities of *lala* women across regions, ages, classes, marital statuses, ethnicities, religions, educational backgrounds as well as sexual and gender identifications in China. Women with bisexual identification and biological women with transgender identifications are two emerging groups whose voices are gaining in the *lala* community. The development of local *lala* communities is also highly varied in different cities and regions. There are well-developed and visible *lala* communities and organizations in metropolitan centres such as Shanghai and Beijing. There are also plenty of *lala* women in smaller cities or counties struggling to connect with each other through less sophisticated social networking tools such as QQ. The regional discrepancy of *tongzhi* community development is significant. Working together with *lala* women from other parts of China extended the physical boundary of my primary research field. Those experiences directed me to look into the specific situations of *lala* women in different regions, and more importantly, to see a bigger picture of the mechanism of public and private regulations at work on *lala* women in China. The participants in my research can be further specified as women with the social and cultural backgrounds enabling their access to local *lala* communities. Their experiences can be referential to those who also live in cities of similar scale or those who are facing similar challenges from family and marriage. For detailed information on the major informants in this project, refer to the appendix "Profiles of Key Informants".

The political engagement of this research project started with an urge to document lesbian lives and emerging *lala* communities in China. Female homosexuality, bisexuality, FTM transgenderism and female *tongzhi* communities in China are persistently under-represented in both public discussions and academic studies. Full-length studies of the homosexual population in China first began in the 1990s. Early studies focused predominantly on the male homosexual groups in urban China (Zhang 1991; Li and Wang 1992; Chou 1996, 1997, 2000; Rofel 1999). There was only occasional or brief mention of female homosexuality in those publications or studies conducted in the 1990s (Ruan 1991; Liu 1992; Pan 1995; Evans 1997; Chou 1996, 2000; Li 2002a, 2002b). Ruan Fangfu, Zhang Beichuan, Li Yinhe and Lisa Rofel have mentioned the difficulties in accessing and interviewing women with same-sex relationships in China. It demonstrates that at least until the 1990s, female homosexuality was both invisible as a social issue and a distinctive social group. In her book published in 1997, Harriet Evans comments that having "very limited access to information, advice and support, few outlets for social activities, and living in constant fear of discovery, homosexuals are effectively denied a voice in public discourses about sexuality." They are merely subjects that are most often "talked to, or talked about" (Evans 1997, p. 209). Evans expresses her concern over the othering of homosexuals in China—where homosexuality is always viewed as deviant or as a form of illness. Homosexuals are most often positioned as objects of academic or scientific studies, and in other cases, as subjects in need of public sympathy (Zhang 1991; Liu 1992; Li and Wang 1992). In the last decade, we can see a growing body of works on sexuality produced by local Chinese scholars in China (Liu 2000; Pan and Zeng 2000; Ma 2003; Fang 2005a, 2005b; Liu and Lu 2004; Pan et al. 2004; Pan and Yang 2004; Ma and Yang 2005; Pan 2005; Sun, Farrer and Choi 2005; Zhou 2006, 2009; Pan et al. 2008; Guo 2009; Ma 2011). These studies on Chinese sexuality produced in China after 2000 can be divided into two groups: extensive quantitative or qualitative studies of sexual behaviour among different social groups, and specialized studies of previously silent or emerging sexual practices or groups in post-reform China. Among them, sociological and legal studies of marginal sexuality represent the two most rapidly growing areas in Chinese academic scholarship in the field. Emerging sexual groups, sexual practices, new cultural representations and legal issues have become popular academic subjects. However, with the growing number of local sexuality studies, the risk of "misrepresentation and distortion" as pointed out by Evans is still present in publications after 2000. In most studies, the framework of analysis and the assumed positioning of researchers are predominantly heterosexual. Sexually marginal groups such as sex workers are still under the risk of being objectified in the name of academic investigations. Recent studies of *tongzhi* in China, published in either Chinese or English, have covered cultural representation of same-sex desires in literature, cinema, cyberspace and studies of local *tongzhi* communities and culture (He 2002, 2010; Sang 2003; Sun, Farrer and Choi 2005; Chen and Chen 2006; Kam 2006, 2010; Li 2006; Rofel 2007; Eng 2010; Engebretsen 2009; Kang 2009; Ho 2010; Kong 2010, 2011). The number of studies or articles of female homosexuality in China has increased in recent years. But it is still significantly fewer than those on male homosexuality. Understanding of the newly emerging *lala* communities in China is extremely limited. Geographically, current research studies on gays and lesbians in China tend to be restricted to Beijing, the capital city of China, and few studies extend research to other parts of the country. One of the first book-length studies of lesbian culture in China is Tze-lan D. Sang's *The Emerging Lesbian: Female Same-Sex Desire in Modern China*, published in 2003. The book traces female same-sex desire in Chinese literary texts that were produced from pre-modern to post-Mao China. It includes a brief field observation of "young cosmopolitan lesbian subjects" in Beijing in the late 1990s. According to Sang, the women she met were "spirited, confident lesbian-identified women in their early twenties who called themselves *tongzhi*", and they had just started to communicate via the newly available Internet (Sang 2003, p. 171). The term "*lala*" was not used at that time. Another more recently published book on gay and lesbian subculture in China also offers a glimpse into lesbian life in Beijing, as well as limited analysis of emerging *lala* communities and politics (Ho 2010). Anthropologist Elizabeth Engebretsen (2009) conducted a comprehensive field study on the *lala* communities in Beijing by documenting the everyday life strategies *lala* women used to cope with the pressure to marry. It appears that ethnographic studies of women with non-normative sexualities or gender identifications in contemporary China, and culturally sensitive analysis of emerging *tongzhi* politics are critical for the present stage of sexuality studies in China. They are also important for the production of grounded knowledge of local *tongzhi* communities and everyday life practices of individual actors.

Book Structure

The book consists of five chapters and a conclusion. The opening chapter maps out the current scene of local *lala* communities in Shanghai and the social backdrop against which those communities and activities emerged. The following chapters examine the public discourses and popular understandings concerning *tongzhi* and homosexuality in post-reform China. In the past two decades, China has been characterized by a rapidly transforming social landscape and shifting paradigms of everyday surveillance of people's private lives. Understandings towards self and aspirations of life have also been undergoing rapid transformation, especially among a generation of people whose everyday existence is much more mobile in terms of both geographical distance and emotional attachment. This poses new opportunities and challenges to people who aspire to lifestyles that deviate from the social norm. In addition, the formation of *tongzhi* community in post-reform China has vastly transformed the lives of people with non-normative desires and gender identifications. The book discusses in detail the impacts of those current public discourses and the emerging *tongzhi* communities on individual *lala* women and how they respond to those new changes and the demands of social conformity. The book concludes with an analysis of a predominant politics in *tongzhi* communities in China. I have named it "the politics of public correctness". It is nurtured in the specific social and cultural context of post-reform China, and at the same time, is a response to the emerging challenges and opportunities presented to *tongzhi* individuals and community at this very historical juncture.

Chapter 1 maps out the growing terrain of *lala* communities in Shanghai. I discuss the possible social, political and cultural influences that have contributed to the rapid development of *tongzhi* communities in contemporary China. Specifically, I provide an overview of the local *lala* communities in Shanghai between the years 2005 and 2011.

Chapter 2 examines the changing public discourses of homosexuality during the economic reform period. They have profoundly transformed the ideological obligation governing public representation of homosexuality in previous decades. Homosexuals are increasingly constructed as a distinctive social group to be publicly scrutinized and regulated. Among the developments of this new public interest, we have seen the rapid growth of *tongzhi* communities both on cyberspace and offline spaces. Together with the general public and experts from different domains, the *tongzhi* community is keenly engaged in the formation of new public discourses on homosexuality.

Chapter 3 looks at *lala* women in their private lives at a time when *tongzhi* communities are becoming increasingly accessible and the public awareness of homosexuality is significantly increased as compared with the past decade. I specifically examine the pressures of marriage and the ways by which *lala* women negotiate their non-normative gender and sexuality under the powerful rhetoric of family harmony and filial piety and within a culture that ideologically rejects women as active and legitimate sexual subjects. I also look into how "silence" and "tolerance", as culturally specific forms of homophobia, work to regulate *lala* women in family and marriage.

Chapter 4 discusses the various ways that *lala* women use to cope with the pressures from family and marriage in their everyday lives. In the first part, I focus on the interactions between *lala* women and their natal families; and in the second part, I focus on the situation of married *lala* women and how they accommodate their same-sex relationships and heterosexual marriages.

The last chapter examines dominant *tongzhi* politics in China. The formation of *tongzhi* communities has created a gap between an increased public awareness of homosexuality and the denial and silence of homosexuality in individual families. This existential rupture caused by the public/private divide has given rise to a culturally specific *tongzhi* politics in China, which I term "the politics of public correctness". It refers to a logic of normalization that seeks to promote a "healthy" and "proper" image of *tongzhi* in order to acquire social and familial recognition, developed as a response to the changing forms of oppression and opportunity of *tongzhi* during the reform era. The most articulate expression of this politics is the practice of "cooperative marriage". I look into the social and political context within which the politics of public correctness developed, and its impact on individual lives and the *tongzhi* communities in China.

This book is an extensive qualitative study of the *lala* communities in Shanghai. Through engaging in participatory ethnography as a Shanghai-native and *lala*-identified researcher, I provide an account of the formative stage of the local *lala* community in Shanghai and the everyday life struggles of its first-generation participants. Given the diversity in geography, culture, and in the social and economic fabric of China and the underlying unease these differences often embody, it is neither possible nor productive to deliver a macro analysis of *tongzhi* that addresses all internal differences within China and within local communities. Therefore, I specify my project as an ethnography of women with same-sex desires in urban China during the formative period of *tongzhi* community. It is also a research project that is informed by my participation in *tongzhi* communities outside Shanghai. The following part is a reflective discussion on methodology and my positioning as both a researcher/community member and an insider/outsider.

Notes on Methodology

This book is based on an ongoing research started in 2005. Between 2005 and 2010, I carried out a number of field visits to Shanghai and conducted face-to-face interviews and extensive participant observation. The duration of visits ranged from a few days to more than one month. I conducted formal recorded interviews with twenty-five self-identified *lalas* in Shanghai and a number of informal, unrecorded exchanges with *lala* women whom I met in different occasions. I entered the *lala* community in Shanghai first through a local organizer. She introduced to me some of the research informants, and later through mutual referrals, I came into contact with other informants. A number of them were introduced to me through different community activities. I remained in contact with some of the major informants after the first interviews to document changes in their lives and in the local *lala* communities.

Most interviews were conducted in *putonghua* and a few were done in the Shanghai dialect or Cantonese, according to the language preference of individual informants. On average, a single interview lasted one to two hours. For some informants, a second interview was conducted to gather updated information about their lives and to follow up on topics that were unfinished in the first meeting. In a few cases, I interviewed couples together. This is usually because they expected to be interviewed together. Other times, I did couple interviews because I wanted interviewees to discuss their relationship. I carried out individual interviews of each partner before or after the couple interview to obtain personal insights and private information.

For participant observation, I attended major community events and social gatherings organized in Shanghai and other cities in China. These included lesbian parties, salon gatherings (*shalong*, topical seminars and sharing), work meetings of *lala* groups, a university lecture on homosexuality, a country-wide queer film festival, queer art exhibitions, *tongzhi* conferences, workshops, training camps and casual social gatherings. During one of my field trips to Shanghai, I shared an apartment with a group of *lala* women. I took part in their day-to-day lives and social gatherings with *lala* friends. I also participated in the oral history project of Shanghai *Nvai* Lesbian Group to document lives of *lala* women in Shanghai, acting as an academic consultant and instructor of workshops for volunteer helpers in the project.

Research Positions

It is both my political *and* academic motivation to contribute to ethnographic details and field-derived analyses of lesbian individuals and communities in urban China. In order to obtain in-depth ethnographical information, I needed to first build up mutually trustful rapport with informants. In this respect, my gender, ethnicity, community identifications with informants and my language ability proved to be productive in rapport building. These shared identities also allowed me a relatively easier entry into the field. It is common that in feminist ethnographies and participatory research on minority populations, a gatekeeper is usually a key source in opening doors to other leads. I got in contact with a major organizer of the *lala* community in Shanghai through my personal network of Chinese lesbian communities in Hong Kong and the United States. Throughout my research, I relied on this key person in the local *lala* community as a significant source of information and as a trustworthy guide to the community.

In the early stage of my research, I introduced myself to informants as a graduate student from the Chinese University of Hong Kong and a member of the lesbian community in Hong Kong. The primary role I took up in the interaction with my informants was a researcher with a background in *tongzhi* activism. I also revealed to informants my native Shanghai background and my ability to speak the local dialect. The fact that we shared the same geo-cultural background proved to be productive in my interactions with local Shanghai informants.

On the other hand, I was aware of the differences between my informants and me. For example, the different accents of *putonghua* we spoke, the different terms and cultural references we used in conversations always reminded me of the fact that we came from different societies. Visible differences between a researcher and her informants such as gender, race, age, class, sexual identity, or in my case, cultural background, can be challenging to deal with during the early stage of rapport building. Being an insider and an outsider at the same time, my strategy was to avoid any false expectations from the inform-ants about my knowledge of their society. I always made it clear during early meetings that I had left China as a child and therefore, even though I could speak the language quite fluently, I did not possess knowledge of the country as an insider. The outsider position allowed me to probe further into subject matters that would otherwise be taken for granted between insiders. For instance, the outsider position allowed me to invite informants to explain to me what was perceived to be "common sense" in their local society. By doing so, it also encouraged informants to look at notions of "common sense" in more reflexive ways.

The distinctive features of feminist methodology include an egalitarian research process that values the reciprocality and intersubjectivity between the researcher and the researched (Stacey 1988, p. 22). Yet the intimate knowledge produced from intensive participatory field research also triggers many meth-odological concerns. Among them, the insider and outsider roles of researchers are much discussed in the feminist research tradition. For an insider researcher, which means she studies a culture that is similar to her own, she has to engage in a constant effort to "defamiliarize" herself from cultural practices or values that are "common sensual" to her; while being an outsider, a researcher needs to deal with her ignorance at the beginning, and later, the careful keeping of a sense of strangeness that might wear off during the research process (Acker 2000, p. 194). It is more complicated when a researcher is both an insider and outsider to her research informants, which was the case in my research. In order to generate more insights from this double position, I applied a method of cross-referencing. When sharing common everyday experiences, I would foreground the cultural differences between my informants and me by defamiliarizing their accounts through a productive comparison with similar experiences in Hong Kong. By cross-referencing the two Chinese societies, it sensitized my understanding of the cultural specificities in *lala* women's experiences. On the other hand, in order not to let the cultural gap between us become obstacles to our interactions, I made conscious efforts to study local norms. Taking advantage of my family connections in Shanghai, I took every possible chance of meeting local inhabitants to get insider's knowledge of Shanghai. For example, I learnt much about the marriage norms and culture of Shanghai by talking to local people in casual dinners and meetings. Also, writing field notes was another effective way to familiarize myself with local knowledge and to refresh my insights as an outsider. This technique is especially helpful for any long-term field study. Insights, comments and stories from sources other than my informants also enriched and triangulated my research findings.

Entering the Community

I conducted my first field visit to Shanghai in June 2005, during which I met Laoda (pseudonym), a major organizer of the *lala* community in Shanghai. Laoda was in her late twenties. She had moved to Shanghai from her hometown in another province a few years earlier. At the time I met her, she was running one of the most popular *lala* websites in China.

It was an evening in June 2005 when I met Laoda for the first time after corresponding with her through emails. She asked me to join her for dinner with a few other *lala* women in a restaurant in downtown Shanghai. I was uncertain if Laoda and her *lala* friends would feel comfortable meeting a stranger from Hong Kong. That evening, I wore a necklace bearing a female sex sign as a quiet declaration of my identification with them. Later, I discovered that the trick worked—one of the women later told me they had noticed my necklace, and were able to confirm more of where I stood. This made them feel more at ease with me and also more interested in me personally. When I got to the restaurant, Laoda and a small group of friends were already there waiting for me. She introduced me to her friends as a researcher from Hong Kong. All of us were a bit nervous and shy at the beginning, but very soon the atmosphere lightened up when I took out a book I edited, *Lunar Desire*,[5] which was published in 2001 in Hong Kong, comprising twenty-six love stories written by Chinese women from Hong Kong, Macau and overseas about their first same-sex romantic relationships. I had carried a few copies to Shanghai, intending them as gifts for informants I would meet. They were very interested in the book, and some even began to read it during the dinner. By then, it was clear to all of them I was a member of their group. This made our interaction much easier. The fact that I could speak the Shanghai dialect was another ice-breaking revelation to those who were also Shanghai natives. My Shanghainese background further blurred the insider/outsider boundary. The moments when I opened my mouth and spoke in the dialect always caused a slight uproar in the group, and would significantly change the group dynamics. At other times in my field studies, I was the only person in the group who could speak the local dialect, as many of the participants in the *lala* community came from other parts of China. As a Hongkonger, I was a foreigner to them in most part, as there are manifest cultural differences across the border. Yet my ability to speak the local dialect made me more like an insider of the city than many of them. This hybrid cultural background, together with my lesbian identification, allowed me to merge much easier with *lalas* in Shanghai. The first time I was aware of this multi-directional ice-breaking effect was during that evening with Laoda and her friends.

Our dinner was followed by a "lesbian night" in a downtown bar and a gathering with Laoda's friends in a karaoke place till midnight. The weekly "lesbian night" was co-organized by Laoda's website, *Huakaidedifang* (or *Huakai* in short, 花開的地方), and the ex-owner of "Bar 1088", a once popular lesbian bar in the city, through a contractual deal with the private bar's owner. The "lesbian nights" ran every Friday and Saturday. On these two evenings, the bar would be named "*Huakai* 1088". The combination of "*Huakai*" and "1088" was a synonym of "lesbian bar" to insiders, and both were well-known "labels" in the community. Helpers from Laoda's website sold tickets at the entrance. Tickets were priced at RMB30 each and included a free drink. Certain parts of the bar were allocated as a women-only zone for lesbian night-goers. I met more *lalas* through Laoda at "*Huakai 1088*". The crowd there was mostly in their early twenties, with mixed regional backgrounds. There were women hailing from other cities, who were now working in Shanghai. A few of them worked and lived in nearby cities, and came to Shanghai only to spend weekends with *lala* friends. A few were local residents who would chat in the Shanghai dialect with each other. When we interacted in a group, we all talked in the national language, *putonghua*.

Informants

The key informants of my research were self-identified *lala* women active in the *lala* communities of Shanghai. For individual profiles of informants, read "Profiles of Key Informants". I focused my choice of informants on those who were either employed or self-employed during the time of interview, and at the same time, attempted to stretch the age range as wide as possible. I did this with the view of recruiting informants with a certain degree of exposure in public at work. I wanted to investigate the aspect of social recognition and their existence in the so-called public domains. Therefore, I did not actively search for informants who had never been employed or who had never been involved in the labour market. As such, I did not include school-aged *lalas* in this research. Besides, the problems that young women face in primary, secondary or tertiary institutions concerning their same-sex desires are categorically different, given the different economic and social positions they occupy. Women in their twenties with post-secondary or university education and with a white-collar occupation proved to be the most visible group in the local offline *lala* communities. Those who were most active in community building—such as hotline workers or the organizing members of local working groups—were predominantly women from this age, educational and occupational group. Their regional affiliations varied, but all of them had urban residency. It was significantly much more difficult to find informants who were over thirty, and very unlikely to see any women over forty in public gatherings. One might catch glimpses of women from a senior age group in some lesbian parties in downtown Shanghai. I have met a group of women appeared to be over forty in one lesbian party held in an upscale bar in the downtown area. I was told by other informants that more private and invisible groups made up of affluent, mature *lalas* with professional backgrounds existed in Shanghai. They met each other in private gatherings, and hence, were harder to be seen publicly. Their class and professional backgrounds required a more discreet socializing style. I was unable to get in touch with any of them.

It is not difficult to find that women who were the most visible and accessible in the *lala* community in Shanghai shared some common demographic characteristics. This is also reflected in the profiles of informants in this research. They were mostly in their early to late twenties. They were economically independent, with a university or at least post-secondary education background. They either held a white-collar job, mostly in private corporations, or were self-employed. They were predominantly urban residents. Many of them were living away from their home cities and families, and were working in Shanghai. Most of them had an independent living space, or could afford one if there was a need. Most of them were unmarried. They were a group of women who had benefitted the most from the economic reform and social changes that had occurred in the recent two decades. The social, economic and sexual freedoms they were enjoying were privileged ones that could not be generalized to women from other social and economic groups. The predominance of women with these demographic characteristics in this research is reflective of the most visible and accessible group in the *lala* communities in Shanghai. However, their voices, though dominant, should not be taken as the only one for the entire community.

Chapter 1
Lala Communities in the Shaping

Shanghai is a city of desires. For hundreds of years, it has been a metropolis of commerce and trade, adventure and entertainment, sex and desires. The old Shanghai in pre-1949 had been dubbed as the Paris in the East, the Hollywood in the East and a paradise for adventurers. It was in this coastal city of China that entrepreneurs, opportunists from all walks of life, movie stars, socialites, pleasure seekers, well-known prostitutes, politicians, writers, artists, and manual labourers from rural areas all conglomerated. It was romanticized as a city where one could turn dreams into reality and desires into practice. These were the more popular ways of narrating old Shanghai. Even the generations born after the establishment of the so-called "new China" took pride in the city's glamorous past. The nostalgic sentiment was common among local Shanghai residents in my childhood in the 1970s. Old people lived on memories, while the younger generations continued the city's legend through a sense of pride nurtured by a collective nostalgia. Migrants from all over the country were attracted to this city by its legendary past and its present economic opportunities. After 1949, Shanghai bade farewell to its capitalist glamour and retreated, as a monotonous socialist city, into relative obscurity. It was not until thirty years later that Shanghai restored itself as a city of desires and dreams. In 2005, the year I started my research, Shanghai had again transformed into a migrant city, with people flocking in from all over the country, in pursuit of their myriad desires and dreams.

The Predecessors

There is a widely circulated anecdote about a group of women labelled the "mirror-rubbing gang" (or Rubbing-mirrors Party, *Mojing Dang* 磨鏡黨), who were known for their same-sex sexual practices and community bonding in late nineteenth-century Shanghai. Their stories can be found in many early literary and historical writings about the city. Ruan (1991) mentions this unconventional group in a chapter on homosexuality in his book *Sex in China: Studies in*

Sexology in Chinese Culture, one of the few early academic works in the 1990s on female homosexuality in China:

> . . . the "Mojing Dang" ("Rubbing-mirrors Party") was active in Shanghai in the late nineteenth century. It was said to be a descendant of the "Ten Sisters", which a Buddhist nun had founded several hundred years earlier in Chaozhou, Guangdong (Canton) province. Members of the "Ten Sisters" lived together as couples. The[y] refused to marry, and some even avoided marriage by committing suicide. A few are rumoured to have killed their husbands so that they could maintain their lesbian relationships. The nineteenth-century Rubbing-mirrors Party was also led by a Cantonese woman and lasted about twenty years. It had approximately twenty members, including three who were mistresses of wealthy men, one who had never married, and more than a dozen rich widows. They attracted new members through their knowledge of sexual technique. (p. 136)

The story of the mirror-rubbing gang is one of the literary anecdotes of old Shanghai enduring in popular imagination. The term *"Mojing Dang"* entered the everyday lexicon of the general public as a euphemism for women with homosexual practices. It carries a negative and mocking undertone. As one of the early and most vivid images of women with same-sex desires and practices in modern Shanghai, it shows how sexually "deviant" women, as defined by the dominant heterosexual male-active/female-passive model, are continually demonized by mainstream discourses.

Almost a century later, I arrived in the same city where the legendary women gang had once blatantly lived out their desires. There was now a visible community of sexually identified women. The emergence of this community was not so much a continuation of the practices of its notorious predecessors as it was a development actualized by the cross-regional connectedness of LGBTQ identities, communities and the social transformation in post-reform China. One major organizer of the Shanghai *lala* community told me that one would always find women in same-sex relationships in the city or elsewhere in China—the difference was whether these individuals or groups were visible to the public, or were themselves aware of each other. Viewed together with the legend of *Mojing Dang* and other forgotten or unrecorded existence of women with same-sex desires and practices in the history of China, therefore, I would say that a set of historically and culturally relevant questions to ask were: What are the social forces that have led to the emergence of sexually and politically identified communities in contemporary China? How would new forms of sexual networking and collective identifications impact on non-normative sexual subjects in both private and public domains? What kind of changes, conflicts or transformations will be introduced into the current configuration of social relationships in China? If a new subjectivity leads to new longings and imaginations of life trajectory, what evolving forms of intimacy or lifestyle will result from a *tongzhi* subjectivity? And what would the possible social and political implications of emerging forms of same-sex relationships be to *tongzhi* communities and society in general?

It is beyond this research's scope of investigation to go deeper into the history and the cultural heritage of women's same-sex community in Shanghai. In the following, I outline possible historical and cultural influences that may have contributed to the rapid development of *tongzhi* communities in contemporary China.

Cross-regional Flow of *Tongzhi* Cultures

The emergence of *lala* communities in contemporary China and their rapid development owe much to the more established *tongzhi* cultures in Taiwan and Hong Kong, and to a lesser extent, to the lesbian and gay cultures in Western societies. This is particularly true of *lala* women in China born after the 1980s. The availability of the Internet for popular use in the late 1990s sped up tremendously all kinds of informational flow across borders, including lesbian and gay cultures. The implications of these informational flows were multifold. First of all, information on globalized lesbian, gay, bisexual and transgender, queer identities, communities and movements accessible through the Internet enabled social networking and information exchange, and resulted in international, regional and local mobilization efforts. Cultural learning and assimilation among *lalas* in different Chinese societies happened in regional or intercity *tongzhi* events. One example of such informational exchange is the "*Lala* Camp". It was first held in a coastal city in Guangdong, in 2007. The three-day camp, later developed into an annual event, assembled lesbian community organizers, veteran LGBTQ activists and scholars from Hong Kong, Taiwan and North America to engage in cultural and political dialogue with local community members in China. The camp represented a historic moment of trans-regional networking and exchange among lesbian, bisexual and transgender communities across the three Chinese societies concerned and also with overseas Chinese or Asian LBT organizations. It led to the birth of an encouraging number of new local *lala* groups in different cities in China.

He Xiaopei, one of the prominent lesbian activists and scholars in China, gives an extensive account of the contemporary history of female *tongzhi* in China in *Talking about Their Love: An Oral History of Women Who Love Women in Shanghai I* (她們的愛在說——愛上女人的女人・上海・口述歷史（一）) (2008). She reveals many real-life accounts of women with same-sex relationships in the pre-identity and pre-community period of China. She argues that female *tongzhi*, defined as women with same-sex desires, have always been around in China, echoing the views of a community organizer whom I talked to in

Shanghai. It is the formation of communities that has made female *tongzhi* in China more visible to society, to each other and to the world. She also relates the formation of *lala* communities in China to the cultural interflow between Taiwan, Hong Kong and China,

> The word *"lazi"* spread from Hong Kong to mainland China and became *"lala"*. Right now in China, there are *lala* websites, *lala* meeting places, *lala* bars and *lala* communities that have become part of *lala* organizing and *lala* activities in general. Therefore, the emergence of the word *"lala"* has not only enabled *lalas* to identify with their own sexual identities, but more so, has given *lalas* an identity with which to build their own communities, to gather and to reach out to more *lalas* for new activities and for organizing such activities. (p. 192; original text in Chinese)[1]

During the pre-Internet period, before the mid-1990s, it is possible that there existed a small-scale circulation of lesbian and gay cultural texts from Taiwan and Hong Kong in cities where contacts with foreigners were available. Lesbian and gay subcultures from Taiwan and Hong Kong were also brought in by individual visitors to China during the 1990s. Individual contacts were an important and major source of information for people in pre-Internet China to learn about lesbian and gay cultures in other Chinese societies and in the West. The opening of the Internet to popular use since the mid-1990s has had a phenomenal impact on *tongzhi*. Almost all of the informants in this research have tried to search for information on homosexuality on the Internet. Many early attempts, as recounted by informants, could be traced back to the late 1990s. Most of them searched in Chinese and looked for information specific to Chinese-speaking populations. Language accessibility and cultural proximity are two major factors for the heavy borrowing from the *tongzhi* cultures of Taiwan and Hong Kong, as well as from a few academic texts on homosexuality written by local Chinese scholars that were circulated on the Internet.

We can identify many aspects of influence of Hong Kong and Taiwan on local *lala* cultures in China. For example, the identities of *"tongzhi"* and *"lala"* were first adopted and developed from local terms used in Hong Kong and Taiwan respectively. The study done in Shanghai by Sun Zhongxin, James Farrer and Kyung-hee Choi (2005) on sexual identities among men who have sex with men investigated the relationship between cultural flow and gay culture in China, and how localization took place in the daily usage of borrowed identities. Models of community building, organizing and forms of lesbian socializing have also been significantly influenced by Hong Kong and Taiwan through individuals or organized exchanges between the two regions and China. For example, the most popular lesbian party in Shanghai at the time of my research (2005) was organized by a woman from Taiwan. In addition, many cultural texts such as films and video works have been imported from Taiwan and Hong Kong, legally and illegally, and those with Asian queer themes are always in high demand and circulated eagerly in Shanghai's *lala* communities.

The availability of the Internet and the interflow of *tongzhi* cultural texts and discourses from Chinese societies such as Hong Kong and Taiwan, together with the intensifying interactions of *tongzhi* groups and individuals among the three regions, have substantially provided the cultural resources essential for *tongzhi* community building in China. This timely cultural flow and exchange would not have flourished or achieved its optimal impact without the unprecedented social changes that have taken place in China during the post-reform era.

A Changing Society and the Rise of Communities

China's *lala* communities have become increasingly visible since the late 1990s. The rise of these communities has much to do with the political, economic and social changes in the country in the past decades. In the following section, I will briefly discuss the numerous socioeconomic factors that have led to the rise of *lala* communities.

In the past two decades, the increasing geographical mobility of the population have contributed to the emergence of visible lesbian and gay communities in metropolitan and economically more developed cities in China. Individual mobility in China, either geographical or social, has significantly heightened after the economic and social transformations in the late 1970s, and has accelerated since the 1990s. Rural reforms in the 1980s, the set-up of special economic zones in coastal cities, the relaxation of the household registration system (*hukou*), the supply of jobs in the fast-growing private sectors and the introduction of the commercial housing market in the 1990s have brought along fundamental changes to people's public and private lives. These policy changes have significantly weakened direct state control on individuals, which has long been carried out through *hukou* and the centralized job assignment system, or the *danwei* (work unit). In the pre-reform years, mobility between jobs was extremely limited. Population mobility was strictly controlled between cities, and was even stricter between rural and urban areas. The *danwei* of an individual controlled almost every aspect of her/his social and private life, from the provision of housing to the regulation of one's love and family life. Therefore, the opening up of the job market and the concomitant loosening of state control have allowed people to live their personal lives with greater autonomy. The newly acquired geographical mobility has encouraged people from less developed parts of the country to look for jobs in cities. Major cities such as Shanghai are densely populated with job seekers from all over the country. For non-natives, the city can provide them with a kind of anonymity that would be impossible to find in small towns where social networks are closely knitted.

The opportunity to break away from close inspection by family and social networks in hometowns is crucial for people who seek to pursue alternative lifestyles. For many, Shanghai is a place to fulfil their career aspirations and also to follow their desired ways of living. Furthermore, safe meeting spaces for lesbian and gay people as well as relevant information are readily available, making the city one of the most active lesbian and gay centres in the country. For some of my non-native informants, Shanghai is the place where, for the first time in their lives, they turned their long-held desires into real-life practice. However, the newly obtained autonomy in personal mobility and private lives cannot be construed as a total breakaway from state control. Those changes are introduced largely by the state, and are sensitive to new policy changes. It is true that the introduction of market economy, to some extent, has enhanced choices available in everyday life—from daily necessities to lifestyle options. It has contributed to the rise of large cities such as Shanghai and Beijing as major centres of *tongzhi* communities. Such forms of liberalization of everyday lives in China brought about by economic development and consumption, or by neoliberalism, have already been extensively discussed (Rofel 2007, Wang 2003; Kong 2011). The economic reform has also opened up more life options, as well as introduced more acute forms of social inequality in the country. For *tongzhi* communities, increased population mobility and the provision of commercial meeting places are helpful in bringing together previously dispersed individuals. Yet, despite the relaxation in controls, it is important to understand that state intervention is always present, and that the market has developed *with*, rather than *against* state power.[2] While enjoying new forms of freedom created by the market, the *tongzhi* communities in China are constantly checked by the state. Community development is highly sensitive and vulnerable to political changes. Sporadic police inspections of offices of *tongzhi* organizations, forced cancellation of activities by local police (even if they are not politically sensitive) and forced shutdown of gay websites (gay websites are usually under more frequent and severe inspection by the state censorship department, possibly owing to the number of members and visitors and the amount of photos taken in the nude) indicate an omnipresent state regulation over *tongzhi* communities.

Over the past two decade, we have witnessed a paradigmatic change in political control over homosexuality in the country. Within a few years of each other, homosexuality was first excluded from legal prosecution with the abolishment of "hooliganism" in Article 160 of the old Criminal Law in 1997 (which was applied to male homosexual activities), and then from the medical category of perverts in 2001 when the Chinese Psychiatry Association formally removed homosexuality from its list of mental disorders. These two "ideological shifts" have at least enabled more positive representations of homosexuality in official discourses. In particular, they introduced a new discursive space for state experts in different professions to discuss related issues with fewer ideological restrictions. Throughout the 1990s and especially during the later years, a number of publications of sexuality studies which investigated formerly condemned forms of sexual practices and relationships were released to the public. Among them, Li Yinhe and Wang Xiaobo's (1992) study on male homosexuals in Beijing and Zhang Beichuan's (1994) comprehensive discussion of homosexuality from a medical perspective are two important earlier works. These two book-length publications inaugurated the active intervention of experts from medical science and social science in the construction of contemporary discourse of homosexuality. (I will further discuss how these two sources of intervention have affected the formation of contemporary homosexual subjects in the next chapter.) After 2000, publications on alternative sexual practices, sexual health, and sexual education targeting the general public continued to flourish. The proliferation of publications on sexual topics in recent years is developed against a social backdrop of decriminalization and demedicalization of homosexuality, as well as enthusiastic participation of experts from the scientific disciplines in the production of a new sexual morality for post-reform China.

The changing economic and political atmosphere in the past decade is also accompanied by a number of significant changes in sexual morality in urban China. One prominent change is the de-orientation of sex from the social/collective to the private/individual. It is generally agreed that the new Marriage Law in 1981, which allows divorce to be filed on the basis of "a breakdown of affection" between wife and husband, has brought about a shift from collective interests to individual rights in intimate relationships (Evans, 1997; Ruan, 1991; Woo, 2006). Ruan (1991) also believes that the national birth control policy has generated an unanticipated general interest in sexual pleasure once contraception became policy, as it freed sex from the ideological trappings of being merely reproductive. One visible evidence of the changing sexual morality in urban China during the 1990s is the phenomenal growth of the sexual health industry. McMillan (2006) attributes the emerging industry to the government's conscious efforts to create a scientific and civilized discourse on sex, and to regulate sex within a narrative of public interest. In this state-endorsed sexual health industry, sexual pleasure is associated with people's physical well-being. Media representations also testify to a shift in attitudes. Evans (1997) examines the mounting interest in women's sexual pleasure, and suggests that it can be dated even earlier back, to the beginning of the 1980s, when a "greater prominence of discussion about women's sexual pleasure" first appeared in magazines (p. 9). In other words, individual rights—in terms of sexual pleasure and satisfaction—have come to be considered as important as the duty of reproduction, and is consequently promoted as an essential part of the birth control policy.

The change in sexual morality is also expressed in a more tolerant public attitude towards people that were formerly labelled as sexual "deviants", for example, celibate women, homosexuals, and people with multiple sex partners. With an increasing number of women now working outside the *danwei* system, which used to assign unmarried women to an economically, politically and socially inferior position, female celibacy has become more accepted, especially in metropolitan cities. For economically independent women, the stigma of remaining celibate has been significantly lessened, though not completely eliminated. The relaxation of political and social control of "abnormal" sexual subjects due to the changing economic reality and sexual morality is another factor that has made possible the emergence of lesbian and gay communities in urban China.

The Social Sites and Activities of *Lalas*

In the following part, I will provide an overview of the *lala* communities in Shanghai and a brief discussion of the community culture during the period from 2005 to 2011.

Both online and offline *lala* communities can be found in Shanghai. The latter is composed of groups that gather at weekly lesbian parties, bars or cafés (operating on a weekly or permanent basis), *tongzhi* student associations in higher education institutions, organized community activities such as topical seminars (or salons), casual gatherings, hotline services, cultural events, and commercial practices. Some of the offline activities are organized by groups originally developed as online communities. Other commercial activities targeting the lesbian market have emerged in recent years. For example, in 2005, a privately run studio for wedding pictures and studio shots opened, exclusively serving a gay and lesbian clientele. At the time of writing, a café for lesbians is also said to open soon in Jingansi, an expensive downtown district of the city. Merchandise such as accessories, T-shirts with recognizable LGBTQ graphics and chest-binding tops are available on lesbian websites. On the cultural fronts, lesbian novels that claim to be written by lesbian writers have appeared in mainstream bookstores.[3] Independent video works produced by *lala*-identified directors have also multiplied. *Gender Game* (傷花, 2006) by Tracy Ni, a native Shanghai video artist, is an independently produced documentary on Ts[4] in Shanghai. The documentary has been shown at internal screenings held in the *lala* communities of Shanghai, and was also featured in the Hong Kong Lesbian and Gay Film Festival in 2006. *Lala* activity has also grown in the academia. Since 2003, the School of Public Health of Fudan University in Shanghai, one of the top ranking universities in the country, has been offering a graduate course on "Homosexuality, Health and Social Science" (*tongxinglian jiankang shehuikexue*), with funding support from the Hong Kong-based Chi Heng Foundation. In 2005, Fudan University started a general education course on "Lesbian and Gay Studies" (*tongxinglian yanjiu*) for its undergraduate students. Both courses have received overwhelming media attention, and have chalked up a record student attendance compared with other university courses offered.

The emergence of *lala* communities in Shanghai and the rest of China in the late 1990s, apart from the aforementioned economic, political and social factors, would have been impossible without the Internet. The Internet has acted as an accelerator to the emergence of identity-based sexual communities in contemporary China. Almost all my informants have obtained knowledge about homosexuality and community happenings from the Internet. The fact that all of them are urban residents probably explains their ease of access to the Internet. Qi, a twenty-nine-year-old woman from a small town in the south of China, told a typical story of how information and Internet change lives,

> Apart from big cities like Shanghai within the country, some smaller cities, especially those small towns without even traffic lights, or rural villages, basically don't have access to a lot of information. It was only when the Internet became more popular that I could . . . I had heard nothing about [homosexuality]. I was already twenty something, and it was about time for me to start dating guys. When I was a student, I had intimate experiences with other [female] classmates. But we didn't think of it as a big deal, and nobody . . . absolutely nobody could have told us what it was. I wouldn't have gone around asking. There were no books, no Internet—we didn't know what it was. Then we thought of it as a process; we thought that the time would come for us to date men and to prepare for marriage. That's it. Until I . . . I feel very lucky that I came across the Internet after I broke up with my boyfriend. I have always felt that I'm very fortunate, otherwise I would have married him for sure. If I found out about my identity only after I got married, can you imagine how hard it would all be, recalling all my memories with my classmates? That's why I feel that access to information and communication are very important."[5]

This is especially the case in the late 1990s, when the Internet service opened up to popular use. Message boards of popular BBS websites became a first point of convergence for homosexual subjects in the country. The most frequently mentioned BBS website among my informants was *Tianya* Community (天涯社區). Launched in 1999, *Tianya* Community is one of the most popular social networking websites in the country. It supports a subtly named message board on its website—*Yilutongxing* (一路同行, "Walk Together")—as a reference to homosexual people. The message board is still active and running in 2012 at the time of writing.

By the early 2000s, there were three major lesbian websites, *Shengqiuxiaowu* (深秋小屋, "Cottage in Deep Autumn"), *Aladao* (阿拉島, "Our Island") and *Huakaidedifang* (花開的地方, or *"Huakai"*, "Where the Flowers Bloom"), all of which were founded by *lala*-identified women based in Shanghai. *Shenqiuxiaowu* has since gradually developed into an online literary community celebrating women's literature and creative writing. *Aladao* is the most enduring first-generation lesbian website in Shanghai. Its founders being a local lesbian couple, the site demonstrates a more pronounced local Shanghainese identification. *Huakai* is a lesbian website targeted at *lalas* all over the country. Its founder, Echo, moved to Shanghai in 2003, and since then, has based her website and offline community networking in Shanghai. *Huakai* engaged message board administrators (*banzhu*) from different cities. At the time of my research, *Huakai* was the most popular lesbian website in the country. In 2005, it had over 40,000 registered members. It closed in 2007 for personal and financial reasons.

The cyberspace has dramatically changed the lives and ways of interaction for people with same-sex desires in China. Since the late 1990s, identity-based lesbian and gay communities have developed in various cities in just a few years' time. For all my informants, the memory of how they first got in touch with other lesbians in the country usually did not hark back to too long ago. A few of them had only gotten to know other *lalas* a few months before the interviews. Within a decade of the emergence of the cyberspace, we are seeing individuals being easily connected, and online and offline communities developing at rapid speeds. In 2008, there were hundreds of lesbian and gay websites operating in China. The number continues to grow rapidly today.

The moment one discovers people like us on the Internet can be as overwhelming as it can be inspiring. The thought that "I'm not the only one" has the positive effect of nurturing an awareness of a collective existence. The Internet has provided a relatively safe space for *lalas* to search for and connect with each other. It has not only encouraged the formation of online lesbian and gay communities, but has also paved the way for the establishment of communities of greater visibility in the offline world. The Internet remains the most important medium of social networking for lesbian and gay people in China. It is particularly useful for those who cannot risk exposing their sexual orientation in the offline world.

Despite all its merits, the Internet is not an all-welcoming public space. Access is not available to everyone. Internet use in China varies across gender, age, education, income, occupation and location (predominantly in cities). According to a study on Internet use in China in 2005, the year I started my research, Internet users were predominantly male (57.2%), aged 16–24 (87.8%), not married (77.2% of this group were netizens), had university education or above (almost 90% of this group were netizens), earned a monthly income of more than RMB2,000 (67.7% of this group were netizens), and held occupations as teachers, researchers, or managers in state, private or foreign enterprises (over 80% of this group were netizens).[6] Therefore, the majority of netizens in China at the time were young, unmarried men with university education and who earned an income above the average level. As suggested by these results, it has been difficult for the cyber *tongzhi* communities in China to reach individuals who are economically, technologically, occupationally, culturally and geographically deprived of Internet access. Regardless of gender, netizens in general were mostly from the more educated and well-off classes. This has in turn reflected in the demographic composition of offline *lala* communities, which are usually developed and maintained by social networking on the Internet. The restriction of Internet access and use has led directly to the over-dominance of women with certain economic, educational, occupational, regional (predominantly urban), and marital backgrounds in offline *lala* communities.

Nor is the cyber world risk-free to its users. The greatest threat for lesbian and gay netizens in China is the possible exposure of their actual identities to their family and colleagues. The threat of exposure has been used to manipulate lesbian and gay people, in both online and offline situations, as blackmailers are well aware of the devastating outcomes which exposure can lead to in one's family, social and work lives. Cases of gay blackmailing in cyber communities have been discussed on online forums and offline gatherings. In a typical case of Internet blackmailing, the offender asks for cash reward in exchange for not exposing the victim's sexual orientation or her/his engagement in gay communities to her/his family, school or workplace. The fear of exposure and the prevailing social prejudice against homosexuality usually deter the victim from seeking help through formal channels such as the police—which can itself turn into a possible source of harassment. The absence of recourse is exacerbated by the lack of legal recognition and protection of homosexual people in China. Bringing forth the case to the police or the legal institution may end up laying the victim open to new risks. As long as homosexuality is socially stigmatized and institutionally discriminated against, the threat of exposure will always be there.

The bar or party community has existed in Shanghai even before the advent of online networking. The earliest bar frequented by *lalas* in the city, as recounted by informants, was *Baifenzhibashi* (百分之八十, "Eighty Percent"), which operated in 1998 in one of the hotels in downtown Shanghai. A small group of *lalas*, fewer than ten in number, gathered there regularly. More often, informants who were bar-goers in the early years (that is, before 2000) told me they usually hung out in a few gay bars in downtown areas. One of the most popular gay bars (still in business and having moved to another location in the downtown area at the time of my research) was "Eddy's 1924" located inside the People's Square at the heart of the city. Opened in 2001 and owned by a gay man, it is one of the first well-known gay bars in Shanghai. Its central location boosted its popularity. Informants told me they used to hang out in Eddy's with gay friends, or just went there out of curiosity. Together with other less popular establishments in the late 1990s, gay bars were the only public spaces available for *lalas* to hang out and meet each other face to face.

Regularly held lesbian parties started to appear in the city in the early 2000s. Commercial cooperation between private bar owners and party organizers (usually *lala* identified) in the form of *baochang* (包場)—leasing out the venue for parties under contract or verbal agreement—has been the most popular form of organizing lesbian parties. The *baochang* agreement usually requires the party organizer to hold lesbian parties during the weekends, usually on Fridays and Saturdays. The bar owner and the party organizer shares the revenue from each party ticket sold and from the overall consumption of drinks and orders from the menu during the party. In the summer of 2002, "Bar 1088" became one of the first establishments to start the practice of cooperating with lesbian party organizers to hold lesbian nights every weekend. The following year, the lesbian nights were brought to a halt despite their sweeping popularity.[7] Such popularity turned the label, "1088", into a synonym for *lala* community in Shanghai. The extent of the label's influence and reach was such that a website was set up under the same name. The virtual 1088 was as popular as the offline one. In late 2004, the owner of Bar 1088 sold her business shortly after the bar stopped hosting lesbian parties. She then became a "nomadic" lesbian party organizer, co-hosting weekend lesbian nights at a quiet, downtown bar (with no dance floor and playing soft music instead) with the website *Huakai*. This came to be known as the "*Huakai* 1088" party, which began in 2005 and ran for two years.

Lesbian parties are always advertised by word of mouth in the community, or through online postings on the message boards of gay and lesbian websites. The nomadic nature of these parties makes partygoers very dependent on their connection with the organizers. In other words, since it is hard to find a permanent location, it is essential for organizers to maintain a good connection with their clientele. The most talked about reason I have heard for why organizers have to change locations is disagreement with bar owners, which can stem from different views on how to run the party, or from unsatisfactory attendance rate due to the location or other physical factors of the bar concerned. Rarely is it related to police intervention or shutdown, though those remain legitimate concerns especially with the introduction of such activities as erotic dance, or when the scope of operation exceeds the limit tolerated by the local authorities.

Given the rarity of exclusive lesbian bars in Shanghai, and given the high financial investment and possible political risks involved in running those bars, the informal and relatively flexible partnership between well-connected lesbian party organizers and private bar owners has persisted as the most popular response to the rising demand for quality social gatherings among the younger and economically well-off *lalas* in the city. Lesbian parties also have the advantage of being a profitable business cooperation. The bar can profit from the additional and almost guaranteed *lala* clientele every weekend. The size of these weekend parties can exceed 150 people per night for a medium-sized bar. Furthermore, the commercial party organizers or community organizers can profit from commissions, and more importantly, the opportunity of having a precious space for community networking. Party organizers usually use the same party name even as they host parties in different venues. Partygoers refer to the name of the party instead of the venue that hosts the party. For example, at the time I was doing my fieldwork, the biggest lesbian party in town was the *"Hudieba"* ("The Butterfly Bar"). The party changed locations frequently, but wherever it "landed", people referred to it only as the "Butterfly Bar", rather than by the official name of the hosting venues. *Lala* parties are also promoted via text messages, websites and QQ groups. Supporters will follow well-known party organizers across the city, in a manner reminiscent of nomadic tribes trekking across large swaths of land, in search of an oasis.

The *baochang* lesbian parties have coexisted with exclusive lesbian bars and cafés. But usually due to commercial unprofitability and various personal reasons, exclusive lesbian bars are short-lived. One example is a café called *Hongba* ("The Red Bar"), which opened in 2004. It occupied a prime location just opposite "Eddy's 1924" at the People's Square. The owner of *Hongba* was said to be a *lala*. It was a small, cosy café with a cultural atmosphere. It was at one time popular among *lalas* who preferred a quieter gathering space without deafening music and a huge dancing crowd. However, *Hongba* did not survive into its second year. Some informants told me it closed down because of financial difficulties. Unlike gay bars that usually have a steady flow of customers, lesbian bars are only busy on Saturdays. Many informants agreed that *lalas* are not as economically well-off, or at least not as willing as gay men to spend money in bars. This makes it extremely difficult for an exclusive lesbian bar to survive in Shanghai, one of the most expensive cities in China. This also explains why the *baochang* practice developed as the dominant form of weekly lesbian parties. It requires only minimal cash investment for promotion and in some cases, payment to performers. *Baochang* demands more a well-established community network and connection with local bar owners. Echo, the founder of *Huakai* website and who later became an organizer of lesbian parties, attributed the lack of exclusive lesbian bars also to the social risks faced by *lala*-identified owners. This goes back once again to the threat of being exposed. Echo said even if *lalas* were economically able to run a permanent lesbian bar, they may not want to deal with the social consequences of exposure.

Offline *lala* community activities first started to take shape in Shanghai in the early 2000s. There were lesbian hotlines, outreach volunteer workers, and regularly held salon meetings. The first lesbian hotline in the city was the *Tongxin* Hotline (同心熱線). It was set up in June 2004, and was attached to the more established *Tongxin* gay hotline. The *Tongxin* Hotline—or *Tongxin* AIDS Intervention Hotline (同心艾滋病干預熱線) in full—was a semi-official operation supported by the International Peace Maternity and Child Health Hospital (上海國際和平婦幼保健院) in Shanghai. The hotline office was located inside the hospital. In addition to hotline services, *Tongxin* also offered sexual health consultation, legal consultation and other outreach activities for the homosexual population in Shanghai. Its medical services included free HIV testing for gay men. The hotline also maintained a website and a newsletter in both print and digital versions, offering information on sexual health and other gay related topics. In 2004, the hotline posted a recruitment notice on its website and other gay and lesbian websites, calling for female volunteers for its new lesbian hotline service and community projects. Drawing on its existing resources, which included medical professionals from the hosting hospital and a pool of experienced male hotline operators, *Tongxin* provided training for the newly recruited female volunteers. The first semi-official hotline for female homosexuals in Shanghai was launched in the summer of 2004. One former *Tongxin* lesbian hotline operator told me the number of calls from women was not as many as male callers to the gay hotline. Many of them called from outside of Shanghai, which means they were not local residents. There were also parents and family members of lesbians and gay men occasionally calling in for advice and information. Some called to have a listening ear to their stories. The hotline operators were required to follow the code of practice they had learnt in training, including the policy of only giving objective advice to callers and referring cases with medical issues to the hotline's medical supervisors in the host hospital. One former operator told me it was one of the principles not to *encourage* callers to engage in homosexuality. The hotline adopted a "supportive but not encouraging" (*rentong danbu guli*) stance, especially to callers who were still at school age and economically dependent on their families. The entire *Tongxin* Hotline was shut down at the end of 2005. Many in the community believed that the closure was due to government intervention. Some speculated that the closure was also related to the crackdown of the country's first homosexual cultural festival held in Beijing that same year. Both incidents indicated a possible tightening of government control over *tongzhi* activities. Almost a year later, in 2006, the same group of female volunteers set up another new lesbian hotline in Shanghai—the "800 Free Hotline", funded by the Hong Kong-based Chi Heng Foundation. It offers peer counselling by *tongzhi*-identified operators to lesbians and gay men. The "800 *Lala* Hotline" is operated every Saturday for two hours in the afternoon. It is still in operation at the time this book is written.

In June 2005, the Shanghai *Nvai* Lesbian Group (上海女愛工作組) was founded by a group of some ten self-identified *lala* women who were, at the time, all based in Shanghai. *Nvai* is the first grassroots *lala* organization in the city without official and overseas affiliations. The group operates a *lala* hotline every Friday evening until late night. It organizes group activities, such as tours to nearby cities and celebrations of international LGBTQ events. From 2005 onwards, it has organized a number of salon gatherings for *lalas* on various topics, including lesbian relationships, coming out, and legal issues related to *tongzhi*. The gatherings are usually held in cafés or bars, with entry tickets costing around RMB20. The income is used to pay for the venue and refreshments. Guest speakers are invited occasionally to speak on specialized topics. *Nvai* also carries out cultural projects. One ongoing project is document-ing the oral history of women with same-sex love in Shanghai. *Nvai* carries out oral history training workshops for volunteers. The project has released its first book, a collection of life stories of fifteen women in same-sex rela-tionships, and circulated it internally within the local lala community since 2007. The oral history project was still ongoing at the time when this book was written.

In December 2005, I participated in a salon gathering organized by *Nvai*. The gathering was held on a Sunday afternoon at a bar located in an easily accessible district, and which was rented out to *Nvai* for the whole afternoon. A sign drawn up on paper—which read "salon gathering" in Chinese, and in smaller font size, "*Nvai* Lesbian Group"—was placed at the entrance of the bar. Inside the venue, a large rainbow flag was hung on the wall facing the entrance. Propped up next to the flag was a big piece of cardboard for participants to sign their names. An hour before the gathering was set to start, people began to arrive. They seated themselves on the sofas and chairs set up in the spacious room, where refreshments had been laid out, and chatted until the meeting commenced promptly at two. Two workers from *Nvai* moderated the meeting. The rest of us sat around them in a circle. The topic for the day was "When love begins". Participants were invited to discuss how couples meet and fall in love, and about different kinds of relationships. The forty or so women in the room included newcomers and regular participants. From their self-introductions, I learnt that most were in their twenties, while the youngest was seventeen, and the oldest over forty. Many came with their girlfriends. Some of them came from outside of Shanghai; therefore, as in many other community gatherings, *putonghua* was the lingua franca. Several couples were invited to share their experiences with love and relationships. Their sharings covered a variety of relationship types, including same-city relationship, long distance relationship, *TT* love (that is, two *T*s as a couple), virtual relationship (*wanglian*, relationship developed on the Internet), and underage love (*zaolian*, usually referring to relationships between teenagers). Participants were eager to share. The discussion was lively, and in general, participants were agreeable to each other. When the discussion moved to the topic of virtual relationships, however, it was obvious that participants were divided in their views. One interesting observation as the discussion proceeded was the obvious division by age. Unlike the younger party crowd, the dominant group at these salon gatherings was women in their mid-twenties and over. This dominant group always called the younger generations "[those] born after the 80s", or simply, "kids" (*xiaohai*). In a similar manner, women born in the 80s would label those born after them as "kids". The age difference seemed even more significant than regional difference as a category of inner-group identification. At events such as salon gatherings, age is usually singled out as *the* cause of differences or disagreements over topics that may not be age-specific. The salon session was followed by a group dinner in a nearby restaurant. Some participants went on to sing karaoke after dinner, rounding up a typical evening of a salon gathering. Besides these salon gatherings by *Nvai*, other local *lala* groups such as *Shenqiuxiaowu* have also organized gatherings and seminars on different topics. They usually attract different crowds according to the networks and preferences of the organizers.

Community activities of *lalas* in Shanghai have extended beyond the city's borders. Regional and international networking with LGBTQ groups elsewhere has intensified after 2005, since the founding of local groups. They have been active in connecting with lesbian and gay organizations in and outside the country. During the period from 2005 to 2010, these groups have led participants to attend female *tongzhi* conferences and activities in Beijing, the International Day Against Homophobia (IDAHO) Parades and Pride Parades in Hong Kong and Taiwan, the *Lala* Camps since 2007 (with lesbian organizers and workers coming from mainland China, Hong Kong, Taiwan and the United States), and international LGBTQ conferences in Asia and North America. Community building and rights activism are developing at full speed. There have also been closer cooperative efforts between advocates from medical, legal and academic sectors and the *tongzhi* communities in Shanghai: legal, medical practitioners and academics have been invited to speak in *lala* salon gatherings on specialized topics and to offer support for the communities. A more in-depth discussion of experts' involvement in the building of *tongzhi* communities can be found in the next chapter.

With the development of online and offline communities, social interaction has become much easier for *lalas* in the city. Yet for many, the possible danger of exposure remains a major concern. Most of my informants kept their same-sex desires and relationships strictly secret from their parents and other family members. Some of them could not express their sexualities in their workplaces. Most of the *lalas* I met in community gatherings were closeted in their everyday lives. In order to protect real identities, *lalas* always refer to each other by nicknames or names used on the Internet. There is an unspoken rule in the community not to ask for people's real names. It is considered very rude and intrusive if one asks for the real name of someone the first time they meet. As some social circles are initially developed from the Internet, members still keep the practice of using net names to call each other long after their first meeting. The practice is so strictly followed that some women will even call their girlfriends by net names in public occasions. One informant told me about an "annoying" woman she met at community gatherings, who liked to ask about people's hometowns. She would insist on knowing the exact geographical locations, and would be dissatisfied if only the province was given. Her insistence was interpreted by my informant as an irritating behaviour and an obvious violation of the rule of discretion that is highly valued in the community. The reason to carefully conceal information regarding one's hometown is that these private particulars can easily put the person concerned in danger of exposing her real identity. This is particularly the case for *lalas* coming from small towns where kinship and social networks are so closely knitted that one's personal identity can be easily tracked down. Native Shanghai *lalas* are often just as reluctant to tell others in the community where they work and reside. Their cautious attitude originates from an even more immediate fear of exposure. With their families and primary social networks all in Shanghai, they do not enjoy the same protection of anonymity as non-native *lalas*. Their fear is reinforced by occasional cases of blackmail of *lalas* and gay men that are circulated within the community.

Lala Kinship and Household

As many *lalas* active in Shanghai communities come from other parts of the country, they have contributed to the emergence of a new form of lesbian kinship—the *lala* household. It is a common practice for a small group of close *lala* friends to form a *lala* household, sharing rental costs and providing each other with mutual support.

I stayed in a *lala* household in one of my field visits. This household was made up of four core family members; their respective partners were occasional residents. They consisted of Shanghai natives and women who came from other parts of China. At the time of my stay, they were all in their early to mid-twenties, and had just set up the household. Not only did they live and eat together, they also took part in community activities together. They related to each other in kinship terms. Each member took up a role in the family in the same manner as in the traditional heterosexual family according to their gender/sexual identification (for example, *T* or *P*), personality or their specialization in household chores. The *T* in the family was the father, and the most capable *P* was assigned the role of mother, even though they were not a real couple. The rest of the long-term and occasional residents were daughters to them. At the beginning, they had made up the family roles for fun, but the fact that all of them and their lovers were closeted to their natal families forged stronger bonds among them as an alternative family. They supported each other emotionally and offered each other the kinds of care that were impossible to obtain from their natal families. One example of this kind of support is when family members encounter relationship crises. Family members, by being deeply invested in each other's relationship, can offer comfort and counsel, since many of them cannot share this part of themselves with parents, siblings or even close friends who do not know their sexuality. This support is sometimes also extended to other family members who are living apart. The *lala* family I stayed with had a group of close *lala* friends who functioned as secondary family members. The secondary members were referred to as "cousins" and "nieces". They were very close to the core members, and visits between them were regular and frequent.

A *lala* family performs multiple functions to its members and the *lala* community as a whole. For family members, it provides round-the-clock emotional support and a precious physical space where they can express and live out their sexuality. For members in the community, a *lala* family usually functions like a community centre where they can socialize with each other without the fear of exposure and public scrutiny. In addition to close friendship, *lala* families are bonded by love. Cohabiting *lala* couples who have an independent living space can supply intimate spaces for meeting, which can function as a nurturing ground for *lala* communities. With the increasing mobility of individuals, and as more *lalas* are economically able to live away from their natal families, the number of *lala* families can be projected to increase in metropolitan areas in China. Emerging lesbian kinship in urban China will be a fertile area for further research.

Lala communities in Shanghai are fast developing. Since the late 1990s, communities have emerged rapidly, appearing first on the Internet, later extending to offline spaces, and recently crossing geographical borders to connect with LGBTQ communities outside China. The numerous social transformations in post-reform China have accelerated the formation of identity-based *tongzhi*

communities in urban centres such as Shanghai. Mobility of people and information are crucial to the development of these communities. The availability
of job opportunities away from one's hometown and outside of the *danwei*
system have largely freed individuals from the day-to-day scrutiny of their
families and the state over private lives. *Lala* communities in Shanghai consist
of locals and women from other parts of China. The dominant group is women
of urban origin, who are educated, economically independent, not in a heterosexual marriage, and mostly in their twenties. During 2005 to 2011, community
developments included the founding of the first local grassroots lesbian group,
the Shanghai *Nvai* Lesbian Group, and the inception of two lesbian hotlines,
Tongxin Lesbian Hotline (2004–2005) and the subsequent 800 *Lala* Hotline
(2006–present). Local communities heavily references *tongzhi* cultures in nearby
Chinese societies such as Hong Kong and Taiwan. Interchanges among lesbian
organizations in the three societies have been increasing in recent years. The
Lala Camp, an annually held three-day training camp for Chinese-speaking
LBT organizers in China, Hong Kong, Taiwan and overseas, is a prominent site
of inter-regional exchanges and coalition. It started in 2007, and has since been
hosted in a number of cities in China. It has generated many cross-regional
projects, and has directly birthed a significant number of local *lala* groups in
different parts of China. Alongside the development of larger identity-based
communities, there are smaller *lala* groups formed by friends that function as
families. *Lala* families radiate from the larger community, and function as dispersed nodal points of social networking for members. The various forms of
lala family, its role in relation to the larger community, and how it introduces
new ways of kinship and ways of living among *tongzhi* furnish new areas for
further research.

Chapter 2
Public Discussions

> I fantasized that there would be a place where homosexuals can converse and interact freely. I fantasized having a lover. But fantasy is not real. In reality, homosexuals do not automatically love all other homosexuals. They choose their partners just like heterosexuals. But where can I find them? In this wide world, all homosexuals hide their true identity. It is so much more difficult for a homosexual to find his ideal partner than a heterosexual. I sometimes was tempted to openly seek a homosexual friend. But how can I? I do not think a homosexual person will do any harm to the country and other people. But why can't we openly discuss homosexuality? We should provide ways for exclusive homosexuals to contact one another. I sincerely wish that our country and related governmental agencies could openly show their concern about our problems. (Letter 8) (Ruan 1991, p. 128)

This is quoted from one of the fifty-six letters that Ruan Fangfu, a medical expert in China, received from readers who responded to his article "Homosexuality: An Unsolved Puzzle" (*Tongxinglian: yige weijiezhimi*), published in 1985 in one of the country's popular health magazines, *To Your Good Health*. In the letter, the gay respondent yearns for a space where homosexuals in China can get in touch with each other freely. To him, it is an unattainable fantasy. Twenty years later, the fantasy has almost turned into reality.

Since the economic reform period, many formerly condemned sexual practices have started to surface in public discussions. New terminology, implying new ways of understanding, are being used to relocate non-normative sexual practices to a conceptually neutral position. Terms such as *"tongxingai"* (homosexual love), *"tongxinglian"* (homosexual love or people), *"duoxinghuoban"* (multiple sexual partners), *"hunwailian"* (extramarital love), *"yiyeqing"* (one-night stand) have become some of the fast adopted expressions in everyday as well as formal contexts. This public naming has had the effect of introducing the formerly "private" beings or practices or those that had been confined to the invisible, private spaces into public discussion and regulation; as a result of which, new sexual subject positions are inaugurated by new ways of conceptualization. Harriet Evans (1997) analyses how dominant discourses in

communist China interact with the changing subject positions of gender and
sexuality,

> . . . texts are effective not through their "message", their "content", but
> through the explicit and implicit, conscious and unconscious, positions
> they make available. The "gaps and silences" are as important in shaping
> the interpretative possibilities as the explicit terms of the narrative . . . So,
> with particular reference to China, whether in the constrained ideologi-
> cal atmosphere of the 1950s to the early 1970s, or in the more consumer-
> oriented context of the last ten years, the dominant discourses and the
> practices they inform have established the broad parameters within which
> women and men become gendered and sexualized subjects. Whether or
> not individual persons consciously acknowledged the dominant gender
> categories of these discourses, they also participate in reproducing them
> by making representations and self-representations—both consciously and
> unconsciously—with reference to them. (Evans 1997, p. 19)

Public discourses regulate the visible (and invisible) boundaries onto which
one can project possible forms of life and where one locates oneself in the
changing contours of social acceptability. The changing official representation
of sexual subjects also implies changing forms of social control over sexuality. The new public attention accorded to homosexuals is a direct result of
the drastic changes that have taken place in the social, cultural and economic
aspects in China in the past two decades. The newly acquired geographical mobility, economic freedom and information technology have created a
material reality that enables the practice of alternative lifestyles and the formation of new sexual communities. For the first time, homosexuality can appear
in the dominantly heterosexual public space as an independent category of
people. Lesbians and gay men have even succeeded in creating a public space
of their own on the Internet and later in the offline world.

In the following part, I will map out a few major discursive sites where the
public discussion and representation of homosexuality are carried out in contemporary China.

From Patients to Subjects of Public Health

Experts from different domains have long been major producers of sexual
discourses in China. Among them, experts from the medical, academic and
legal disciplines are the most significant sources of knowledge production on
homosexuality and sexuality in general. During the reform period, there arose
a state-directed interest in sexual science (性科學), promoted as the pursuit of
a new scientific understanding of human sexuality. This new approach was
posited as a revision to the earlier state-imposed silence and restrictions on
public discussions of sexuality especially during the period of the Cultural

Revolution (1966–1976), and was "considered essential to the healthy development of the nation's future" (Evans, 1997). A "correct" and "objective" attitude
towards sex was first introduced and promoted by medical experts in the early
1980s when sexual science was introduced. One of the major areas of investigation was abnormal sexual behaviour and psychology. After a long period
of enforced silence, the study of sexuality in medical science reappeared with
unprecedented enthusiasm. It is generally agreed that the publication of *Sexual
Medicine* in 1982 started a new wave of sexual science studies in contemporary
China. The work is an edited Chinese translation of *Textbook of Sexual Medicine*
(Kolody, Masters and Johnson 1979) published by the Scientific and Technical
Documents Publishing House in Beijing. However, this early major publication has four chapters removed from the original volume. The four omitted
chapters cover topics on rape, homosexuality, sexually transmitted diseases
and sex change. The explanation provided in the "Preface" is that the four
chapters are "not clinically relevant". This reflects the cautious attitude of early
attempts of medical experts in dealing with socially controversial topics. In
1985, the same publication house released the first popular text on sex education, *Handbook of Sexual Knowledge*, written by Ruan Fangfu—then a medical
professor in Beijing—and a team of medical experts. In this booklet, homosexuality is included in the discussion, but is defined as a form of abnormal sexual
behaviour. Both books were popular in sales, and were reprinted many times
to meet the never-flagging market demand (Liu, 2000). These two books from
the 1980s—one technical and one popular—were packaged as scientific texts.
It was a conscious editorial strategy of the publisher to make sure writers did
not step on the ideological "landmines" (ibid.). Packaging the books as scientific texts protected early publications on sexuality from moral and political
charges. In the next two decades, medical publications on sexuality continued
to appear in significant number.

As early as in the first half of the 1980s, articles on homosexuality appeared
occasionally in medical and academic journals. One article titled "Phenomenon
of Homosexuality in the Red Chamber" (*Honglouzhong de tongxinglian xianxiang*)
was published in *Popular Medicine*, a medical journal catering to mainstream
readers. In the article, the author—a medical doctor— discusses homosexuality
with reference to a classical Chinese literary text *Hongloumeng* (or *The Dream of
the Red Chamber*), a widely read literary work written in the Qing Dynasty. The
novel contains descriptions on both male and female same-sex love, providing
the author with a point of entry into the discussion of homosexuality,

> Is homosexuality a disease? One cannot provide a simplistic conclusion.
> We can only say that homosexuals are mentally ill and psychologically
> abnormal. It is because a normal person's psychological condition is often
> pointed towards heterosexuals, in other words, "A pretty girl is wooed by a

> gentleman". For homosexuals to desire someone of the same-sex is a form of
> sexual perversion. But what is the reason for such a psychological change?
> Here it may be a situation of three factors: biological, psychological and
> social . . . If we find that the main reason is due to physiological changes,
> then we should treat it as an illness and provide the proper treatment . . .
> From the point of view of abnormal psychology, the ones who are psycho-
> logically abnormal among homosexual lovers are primarily the effeminate
> husbands and the masculine wives . . . Therefore, they are most likely in
> need of treatment or therapy because they are psychologically abnormal.
> (Zhang 1981, pp. 42–43; original text in Chinese)[1]

The book follows the dominant paradigm of that time of discussing homosexuality in the context of sexual abnormality. Prior to 2001, homosexuality
was officially defined as a mental illness in China. It was treated as a type of
deviant sexual behaviour, and public discussions of homosexuality were consistently conducted in the context of abnormal psychology. Diagnoses and
treatments were available in hospitals for people exhibiting homosexual behaviour. Even after homosexuality was officially removed from the new "Chinese
Classification of Mental Disorders (3rd version) (CCMD-3) in 2001, many
medical experts in the country today still hold onto the belief that homosexuality is a mental disorder. The CCMD-3 retains the category of "self-discordant
homosexuality", which means one who cannot accept oneself as a homosexual,
and hence psychiatric counselling and aversion treatments are still provided
in hospitals. The association of homosexuality with abnormal psychology has
persisted in people's minds even after it was formally dismissed.

Pathologizing homosexuality was dominant in medical writings in the 1980s,
even by sympathetic authors. For instance, Ruan Fangfu's "Homosexuality:
An Unsolved Puzzle" published in 1985 reveals a coexistence of contradictory
stances. In the beginning of the article, Ruan calls for fairer treatment of homosexual people in society,

> Homosexuality is against the nature of living organisms. From a biologi-
> cal point of view, human sexual behaviour is connected with reproduction.
> There is no reproduction between the same sex. The proliferation of homo-
> sexuality among humans will lead to serious problems of reproduction. But
> homosexuals should not be punished or disdained simply because homo-
> sexuality does not lead to reproduction. There are a significant number of
> heterosexual couples (the number no fewer than homosexual ones) who
> are non-reproductive. The society does not blame them for this. In this
> era of family planning, a majority of sexual behaviour has nothing to do
> with reproduction. The society does not blame it, but instead encourages
> it—then why is homosexuality criminalized and blamed for being non-
> reproductive? (Ruan, 1989, p. 14; original text in Chinese)[2]

A few paragraphs later, he shifts to dismiss homosexuality,

> Of course, I am not advocating homosexuality here. Actually, one cannot see the pros of homosexuality especially when homosexuals face a series of social, moral, legal, economic and medical pressures with all sorts of dire consequences. As a result, it is not worthy of advocacy, and in reality, one cannot change a "strict heterosexual" into a homosexual, just as it is impossible to change a "strict homosexual" into a heterosexual. It is not possible to eradicate homosexuality even in countries, ethnic or religious groups where homosexuals are punished by death penalty. What is to be emphasized here is the need to address squarely the issue of homosexuality and to treat it in a reasonable manner. (Ibid.)[3]

In the concluding paragraph, he echoes the dominant discourse of prevention and the marginalizing of sexual deviants for the sake of protecting minors and the family institution,

> "Prevention is key" when it comes to homosexuality: harmonious relationships in the family, good education for children including timely and appropriate sex education, a civilized environment for young people to get to know persons of the opposite sex—all help to reduce the occurrence of homosexuality. (Ibid., p. 16)[4]

Despite its shortcomings, this article was one of the rare few at the time to call for a fairer treatment of homosexuals. Its publication brought about an influx of sixty letters from readers—mostly gay men—responding to the article. The letter quoted at the beginning of this chapter is from one of these gay respondents. Six years later, in his English book *Sex in China: Studies in Sexology in Chinese Culture* published in New York, Ruan exhibits an obvious change in attitude towards homosexuality. In one chapter on the topic, he references his earlier article from 1985, and quotes from some of the letters from his readers. However, he does not mention again the preventive treatment that he had promoted in his earlier article, and instead, shifts to a pro-gay rights stance, criticizing China's repressive policies towards homosexuals. Both articles demonstrate a genuine concern for homosexual people in China, but they employ entirely different narrative strategies and discourses of homosexuality. The first, beginning with a positive recognition and ending with a repressive conclusion, is in line with the official narrative of homosexuality at the time in China. The second adopts a gay rights perspective that is dominant in Western societies. Ruan in his later book even unambiguously calls for a policy change,

> It is time—past time—for the Chinese government to change its policies. Not only must it recognize the rights of gay people and develop educational programmes promoting public acceptance of their lifestyle, it must begin promoting safe sex practices, ultimately preventing the premature deaths of perhaps millions of innocent people. (Ruan 1991, p. 134)

Although he emphasizes the importance of preventive measures for homosexuality in the 1985 article, in his later English publication, he acknowledges the situation as a "sad" one, when twenty-six out of the fifty-six gay men sending him letters asked how they might be healed (Ruan 1991, p. 129). Similar shifts in views or incoherent stances are present in publications by other medical experts from that period, including the works of Zhang Beichuan, a widely respected gay rights advocate. The dominant repressive narrative can similarly be located in Zhang's book on homosexuality published in 1994. The structure of this type of narrative is characterized by a concluding comment reaffirming the need for preventive treatment for homosexuality, regardless of the sympathy shown in the preceding paragraphs or chapters.[5]

Given the unstable political climate, it is understandable why such contradictory opinions on homosexuality were presented in the writings of many sympathetic medical, academic and legal experts. It is in large part a function of the social context—when and where these articles were published, and who their intended audience was. The repressive narrative structure was a dominant style of public discussion of homosexuality during the 1980s, and it has persisted even after homosexuality was depathologized. For instance, Liu Dalin's book on homosexuality in China (2005), which provides an overview of homosexuality in ancient and contemporary China, concludes with a chapter entitled "Prevention of Homosexuality", despite Liu's being one of the most progressive experts of sexology in contemporary China. Perhaps the writers used the repressive narrative model out of political considerations—it is difficult for us to gauge; but most evidently, political consideration was and remains a major factor shaping and defining the form and contents of public discussions of controversial sexual practices and populations in contemporary China.

Following the publication of *Their World: Looking into the Male Homosexual Group in China* in 1992, the first Chinese sociological study of male homosexuals in China by Li Yinhe and Wang Xiaobo, Zhang Beichuan published the first comprehensive medical study of homosexuality, *Homosexuality* (*Tongxingai*), in 1994. Zhang is a medical professional specializing in human sexuality. In the book's preface, he mentions the two reasons that compelled him to write: the inadequacy of homosexuality research and publication in China at that time, and the sufferings of homosexuals due to social prejudice and ignorance. He states clearly that his own views are at odds with homosexuality, but that as a medical practitioner, he is obliged to "understand the reasons and meanings for it [homosexuality] cogently, to thoroughly understand the dangers of its existence, to use scientific methods to actively pursue ways to prevent and to deal with it" (p. 4).[6] Alongside his sympathetic undertone, we can easily identify an echoing with the repressive narrative model of earlier medical writings on homosexuality. This becomes quite obvious as we examine the chapter outline of the book. The ten chapters of the book are, "a history of researches on the phenomenon of homosexuality", "the definitions, the current

state and categorizations of homosexuality", "the practices of homosexuality", "the causes of homosexuality", "the relationship between homosexuality and psychological (mental) illnesses", "the prevention and treatment of
homosexuality", "sexual deviances that are related to homosexuality (sexual
practices)", "sexually derived bodily illnesses among homosexuals", "homosexuality and sexual morality", and "homosexuality and laws on sexuality".[7]
Unquestionably, Zhang is driven by a deep sympathy as a medical practitioner
to engage in a more comprehensive and scientific understanding of his patients.
Another important point to note is that Zhang's book was published before
the official depathologization of homosexuality. This may be a major reason
why the repressive narrative model was adopted, and why homosexuality was
discussed in the context of sexual abnormality. The cover of the book notes,
"homosexuality is a sexual crisis and tragedy entrenched within society",[8]
and states the major aims of the publication—to improve medical and popular
understanding on the subject, to furnish the heterosexual majority with a scientific treatment of homosexuals, and to help homosexual patients enforce their
self-discipline.[9] *Tongxingai* was the first full-length medical publication to speak
directly of and to the homosexual population in China. It was one of the first
attempts by state experts—who have been traditionally a powerful source of
social control over non-normative sexual subjects—to publicly express a sympathetic view towards homosexuals. Zhang's later efforts in lesbian and gay
activism and HIV/AIDS prevention campaigns in China were a continuation
of his earlier endeavours in the demystification and destigmatization of homosexuality. His efforts in different periods were vented through the particular
discourses allowed and accessible at the times concerned.

Against the backdrop of a state-promoted scientism, the medical institution
was vested with the authority to determine what human behaviour is considered to be normal and abnormal, and by extension, whether it is legal or illegal.
One of sociologist Li Yinhe's (2002) male informants—who was serving in the
army during the Maoist era (1949–1976)—showed how the medical institution
intervened in his private life and altered his social status,

> I was caught sleeping with someone of the same sex in the army and got a
> warning from the Party. At that time, I was accused of sodomy. During the
> years from 1968 to 1978, they continued to consider my case as sodomy,
> up until my sentencing . . . I requested for a medical examination, but my
> request was denied by my *danwei*. Later, I sneaked out to Hospital X to get
> examined; that was how I discovered I was a homosexual. Then I went to
> three other hospitals in Beijing for further examinations and was clinically
> diagnosed as one. In 1980, the high court at the provincial level revised my
> sentence, and I was allowed to resume work. But up till now, my party
> membership and the missed work payments have not been reissued. (Li
> 2002a, p. 391)[10]

His medical diagnosis led to a revision of the criminal court sentence:

> Defendant X had been sentenced to a fixed-term imprisonment of two
> years outside of jail under surveillance under the charges of hooliganism.
> The defendant was later dismissed of criminal charges, and the case went
> under review. The latest review of the original sentence confirms that it is
> not a case of criminal offence because X has the sickness of "homosexu-
> ality". Therefore, the original sentencing and subsequent reviews will be
> corrected. (Li 2002a, p. 391)[11]

Although the medical confirmation of homosexuality as a sickness kept this
man from legal punishment, it placed him under a similarly severe system
of social control—one in which he was defined as a patient. Indeed, medical
knowledge is often an effective form of social control; this has been particularly
the case in China where medical professionals play an influential role in the
expert system of social control. The medical organ of social control in China is
discussed by Evans,

> Identification of a range of "abnormal" or "deviant" behaviours (*bu
> zhengchang xing xingwei*) that have been produced since the early days of
> the People's Republic has served to legitimize the values and practices sub-
> scribed to by official medical and professional agencies. When contained by
> a state discourse, as in China, public discussion about "peripheral" sexuali-
> ties functions to support an agenda that corresponds with official interests
> in social control. (Evans 1997, p. 187)

Before the economic reform period, homosexuality was strictly considered a
medical abnormality. During the reform period and after the official depathologization of homosexuality in 2001, homosexuality has continued to be subject
to severe medical intervention. It is still the case now, though the context of
regulation has changed with the introduction of the HIV/AIDS health intervention programmes as part of a state-endorsed project since the mid-1990s.
Since then, much effort has gone into public discussion and studies of the
male homosexual population. In 1995, homosexuality in China was recognized
officially for the first time in a health manual, *Handbook of Health Education*,
which was jointly published by the National Health Education Institute and
the Ministry of Health. One of the booklets in the manual directly addresses
male homosexuals in the country (Pan 2004, p. 253). The publication marked
the first official induction of homosexuals into public discussion, signaling
an end to the era of official denial of the condition. However, by first introducing male homosexuals to the public as agents of HIV, the state created a new
form of stigmatization by associating homosexuals with HIV/AIDS. As Pan
Suiming warns,

> AIDS contagion has itself become a cultural tool in this discussion with
> which the country intrudes into private lives. Moreover, the meaning of

AIDS prevention stretches beyond the publicity materials. It has become a reason for the police and other authorities to harass and to imprison homosexuals. This situation is also a result of an entrenched distrust held by legal authorities and public health organizations against homosexuals. (Pan 2004, p. 257; original text in Chinese)[12]

The current state-imposed sexual health campaign has led to more stringent control of individuals' private lives. By officially reinforcing the association between HIV/AIDS and male homosexuality, the state has also inadvertently encouraged further stigmatization of individuals concerned, making it harder for them to be accepted as normal and healthy subjects. The HIV/AIDS prevention campaign, in opening up public discussion and intervention of male homosexuality, also has impacts on the resource allocation and development of the *tongzhi* communities in China. With funds consistently increasing and skewing towards MSM (men who have sex with men) and sexual health projects for gays, the existence and community development of female homosexuals in China are further being marginalized. This is part of the reason leading to the current development where local *lala* community groups are dependent on more established gay groups for financial and other resources.

Legal Controversies

The most important development concerning homosexuality in the legal domain during the reform period was the removal of sodomy and hooliganism from the revised Criminal Law in 1997. Both charges had been used to penalize male homosexuals in the past. The newly introduced "Obscenity Law" (Article 237) did not mention homosexual conduct. The abolishment of these two crimes was regarded as an official attempt to decriminalize (male) homosexuality. However, it did not mean that homosexual activities in China were since then freed from legal control. Hooliganism, though not as an independent category of crime, was still included in the revised Criminal Law issued in 1997. Its ambiguous definition continues to give grounds for the penalization of homosexuals.[13]

The legal domain is most loaded in controversy and ambiguity in its treatment of homosexuality in China. The major reason is that there has never been any law *overtly* prohibiting homosexuality after 1949. Only an inclusive category of "hooliganism" existed, encompassing all socially deviant conduct at the time. The actual meanings of "sodomy" and "hooliganism" have always been open to arbitrary interpretation by local legal and public security authorities. As Li Yinhe (2006) comments, "the most serious threat to same-sex sexual conduct between consenting male adults comes neither from legal sanctions nor from police arrest in the name of public security, but rather from social prejudice, which was resulted in the arbitrary imposition of administrative penalties and Party disciplinary sanctions" (p. 82). As in the cited case of Li's (2002) male homosexual informant, the legal treatment of homosexual conduct has depended very much on the attitude of individual *danwei* and the extent of intervention by local medical authorities. The nature of administrative penalties is highly arbitrary. Administrative penalties and party disciplinary sanctions exercised through *danwei* and public security system are especially destructive to the individual concerned if s/he relies on *danwei* for the provision of everyday needs, which is still the case for many people in China at present. The penalties directly threaten an individual's political, social and economic survival in everyday life.

Zhang Beichuan, in his book *Tongxingai*, which was published in China before 1997, mentions that male homosexuals were always prosecuted under the charges of hooliganism and sodomy. He offers as illustration a case of police arrest of male homosexuals under the charge of hooliganism in 1988,

> For example, in Hangzhou, around the year 1988, legal authorities arrested more than sixty male homosexuals, citing Article 160 [my note: which referred to "hooliganism"]. The Article states that "group fights, disturbance of public order, grave situations will lead to sentencing to a fixed jail term of seven years or below, detention or community order. Key persons involved in hooligan groups will be sentenced to seven years or more fixed-term imprisonment". (Zhang 1994, p. 633; original text in Chinese)[14]

Zhang also highlights the huge differences in the treatment of male homosexuals in various cities after the mid-1980s, when semi-public and public male homosexual hangouts started to appear on the urban grid (ibid., p. 635). Mass arrests of male homosexuals in police raids of gay nightclubs took place in one city, while in another, male homosexuals gathered at public spaces were "invited" by the police to "talk" about their situations, confidentiality being guaranteed.

Public remarks by authority figures and state organs continue to serve as an important source in understanding the legal treatment of controversial social conduct in the country. Alongside the conception of homosexuality as a mental disorder, the practice of homosexuality has been recognized as a public security issue to be put under the control of criminal law and state authorities concerned. For instance, Zhang (1994) mentions one official remark concerning homosexuality in 1987, "The legal authorities in 1987 stated in response to the legal positioning of homosexuality: 'Due to the social immorality caused by homosexuality, its disturbance to the order of society, its harmful influence on the psychological and physical health of the youth, homosexuality is a form of criminal behaviour'" (p. 633).[15] In 1989, the authority declared that "homosexuality is a behavioural and psychological abnormality [which may] lead to theft, prostitution and murder" (*Renmin jingcha*, or *People's Police*, 1989, pp. 11–12, quoted from Evans 1997, p. 210). It is obvious in this remark that repressive discourses from both medical and legal interpretations were applied to condemn homosexuality. Ruan in his 1991 publication also observes that, "When public figures do speak out on homosexuality, it is usually to condemn it" (Ruan 1991, p. 131). He quotes a public speech on homosexuality by one of the most famous attorneys in China in the 1980s, in which the legal expert supports and justifies penalizing homosexuals administratively and criminally for social and security reasons (ibid., p. 131).

Inconsistencies in treatment of homosexuals by local legal authorities and in the views voiced by officials and experts were common in the economic reform period. At the same time, the debate over whether homosexuality is a criminal conduct has always been carried out in the medical and legal domains. In 2000, the Chinese Ministry of Public Security made a public remark stating that "people [have] the right to choose their own sexuality" (Gao 2003, quoted from Li 2006, p. 83). It is uncertain if this was the first official announcement of individual sexual rights in the country, but undoubtedly it marked a discursive shift in the official interpretation of sexual orientation. The remark invited people to imagine forms of sexuality outside the heterosexual monogamous model. Within a decade, we witnessed a drastic change in attitudes in the public remarks made by legal and medical experts on homosexuality. The social reality after 2000 had already changed significantly from that of the 1990s. In 1991, Ruan had boldly concluded that all public figures in China would speak openly to condemn homosexuality. Ten years later, we were seeing a growing force of legal professionals advocating for gay rights in China. Among them was Zhou Dan, a Shanghai-based legal professional and China's first lawyer to come out publicly, and who is a prominent gay rights figure in the country.

Over time, homosexuality has become increasingly understood as an issue of human rights and as inseparable from legal empowerment. The heightened awareness of homosexuality in the public arena resulted partly from the heated debates in the legal domain during the reform period, and partly from the increasingly open support of some legal experts in the acquisition of equal rights for lesbians and gay men in the country. This supportive legal force is especially visible into the twenty-first century, after the removal of sodomy and hooliganism from the revised Criminal Law in 1997. In China today, the visibility of lesbians and gay men in legal discussions contributes to the public awareness of the legal marginalization of lesbians and gay men. Through these discussions, topics such as sexual orientation and alternative sexual practices and lifestyles are introduced into public dialogue.

One example to highlight in this trend of expert engagement in the gay rights campaign is sociologist Li Yinhe's bold attempt to lobby for same-sex marriage. As the first sociologist in the country to conduct research on male homosexuality and presently the academic spokesperson of homosexuality in China, Li has pushed her efforts further since 2001 by formally filing consecutive petitions to the National People's Congress for the legal recognition of same-sex marriage in China. In her "Petition of the Legalization of Same-Sex Marriage" to the National People's Congress, Li advocates same-sex marriage through four discursive paths: legal, political, public health, and nationalist (Li 2005, pp. 112–114). Legally, Li states that there is no law prohibiting same-sex marriage in China. Politically, the recognition of same-sex marriage will be an indicator of the country's strong human rights status (even better than the United States). Medically, it will be an effective measure to stabilize homosexual relationships, and hence to prevent sexually transmitted diseases. And finally, it is beneficial to the overall societal harmony, and can boost China's national image. Although Li's attempts failed due to lack of positive votes, they demonstrate the increasingly visible and public endeavour of state experts to call for changes in the legal status of the country's homosexual population.

The legal developments and changes in the last two decades have two implications for the country's lesbian and gay population. First, as legal action against homosexual conduct is always directed to male homosexuals, female homosexuality is rarely talked about in public discussions. This has reinforced the existing ignorance about female homosexuality in society. Secondly, it is argued that the decriminalization of male homosexual conduct actually leads to a legal denial of homosexuality. Legal invisibility can be even worse than the previous ambiguous inclusion under "hooliganism" and the crime of sodomy in the old law. This new legal denial has been interpreted by the *tongzhi* communities in China as an indication of further deprivation of legal protection for the population concerned (Jia 2005, p. 12).

The invisibility of female homosexuality in dominant legal discourse bespeaks a much more severe social surveillance of male homosexual activities. In other words, it hints at a heightened cultural anxiety towards male homosexuality. Female homosexuality is culturally considered as less threatening to public security and social morality. However, tolerance and silence do not imply that female homosexuality is socially or legally accepted in China. Occasional media reports about female homosexuals usually tell of murders and suicides. Glimpses of the lives of female homosexuals can be found in police accounts of sex criminals, as in China, cases of female same-sex practices are documented at random. Ruan in 1985 conducted interviews with three women who were imprisoned in the Shanghai Women Delinquents Correction Institution. All of them had participated in same-sex sexual activities and were arrested for both their female homosexuality and other illegal sex practices such as prostitution and promiscuity (Ruan 1991, p. 141). Another more recent and significant legal case, widely reported and termed by the local media as "the first homosexual case in new China", happened in the county of Wuwei in Anhui Province in 1991. The case began when the parent of one of two female lovers filed a "prosecution letter" to the local public security office against the couple, requesting the authority to "severely punish this disgusting phenomenon".[16] The reply from the public security bureau stated that, "[t]he definition of homosexuality and the responsibilities of homosexuality are not clearly stated in current legislation. Under this condition, the questions you have raised can be neglected in principle. It is also not appropriate to use hooliganism as a form of administrative punishment. The way to settle this case will be up to different procuratorates or courts" (ibid., 2005; original text in Chinese).[17] The official remark has been regarded by the public as a first step towards decriminalization of homosexuality in China. The case was the first instance of public legal litigation of a female same-sex relationship. In general, female homosexuality is largely absent in public discussions.

In the post-criminalization era, lesbians and gay men in China are still under the threat of arbitrary administrative penalties, even though the decline of the *danwei* system has reduced the political, social and economic damages and risks of individuals being accused of homosexuality. The absence of any explicit or implicit mention of homosexuality in the revised Criminal Law of 1997 on the one hand has partially released male homosexuals from the fear of being arrested under the crimes of sodomy and hooliganism. On the other hand, it also implies a new legal denial of homosexuality and a consequent absence of legal protection for the population concerned. The emergent legal reform movement of lesbian and gay rights is directly induced by the decriminalization of homosexuality and also by the enthusiastic public and expert discussion of homosexual rights in China.

The Sociological Other

The third major site of public discussion of homosexuality in the economic reform period is the local academia.

As mentioned above, Li Yinhe and Wang Xiaobo published the first book-length sociological study on male homosexuality in China in 1992, based on interviews of male homosexuals in Beijing during the period from 1989 to 1991. The significance of this book is that it was the first sociological study of homosexuality after a prolonged silence in the field of social sciences. However, the book was criticized for heterocentrism and for its otherization of homosexuals. The title of the book, *Their World*, tells a lot about the positioning of the researchers and the relationship between them and their research subjects. In fact, it reflects the overall power dynamics between the heterosexual majority and the homosexual minority in society back then.[18] In this first sociological study of homosexuality, homosexuals were put under heterosexual scrutiny in much the same way as being medically examined. Despite the authors' humanistic concern and call for equal rights, the presence of an authoritative heterosexual voice clearly illustrates the power hierarchy between the researchers and the researched.

Subsequent publications during the same period demonstrate a similar otherization of homosexual subjects. Notable examples are *Homosexuality in China* (1995) by Fang Gang, published in China, and *Black Souls under the Red Sun* (1995) by An Keqiang, which was published in Taiwan. A number of publications about *tongzhi* in China, either written as sociological or personal accounts, also appeared in Hong Kong during the 1990s. Hong Kong sociologist Chou Wah Shan conducted interviews of male and female *tongzhi* (Chou uses "*tongzhi*" in his works) in China, publishing a number of books during the 1990s in Hong Kong. Other personal accounts of male and female homosexuals in China from that period include *We are Alive* (edited by Wu Chunsheng and Chou Wah Shan in 1996), and *Beijing Tongzhi Stories* by Chou Wah Shan in 1996.

Sociological studies of homosexuality in China have proliferated in the twenty-first century. Within a context of fast-growing sexuality studies in social sciences, more and more local researchers and graduate students have begun to study related topics in China. Large-scale surveys on sexual practices have included homosexual practices in different age and social groups, such as those among university students and rural and urban residents (Liu 1992, 2005; Pan 2000, 2004a, 2004b, 2008). Since 2000, universities have been offering undergraduate and postgraduate courses on sexuality and homosexuality. Homosexuality has become popular as a subject in universities and as a topic of student dissertations. It is a common sight to see university classrooms packed with enthusiastic students and even members of the general public whenever homosexuality is discussed.

The above analysis shows how experts from the medical, legal and academic domains occupied a central position in the production of authoritative knowledge of homosexuality in the reform period. Lesbians and gay men in the country also referred to experts for information or consultation of their sexualities, relationships, legal concerns and health issues. In this manner, experts came to take on the role of public spokespersons for the silent population of lesbians and gays in China.

New Possibilities of Private Life

A *tongzhi* cyber public has been taking shape since the late 1990s and early 2000s. Starting up with ambiguously named message boards and chatrooms knowable only to insiders, the *tongzhi* cyber community in China consists currently, as estimated by members of the community, of more than 300 lesbian and gay websites. Within a few years, the cyber community has risen from ground zero, and has been developing rapidly to a size and scope of influence that would take decades for an offline community to accomplish. *Tongzhi* cultures that have been developing in nearby Chinese societies, Taiwan and Hong Kong, have all at once been assimilated, with the effect of spawning rapid development of localized *tongzhi* identities and cultures. This has given rise to a highly condensed process of community building, cultural formation and transformation.

In 2005, the year I started fieldwork in Shanghai, everyone I met had only entered the local *lala* community very recently—none of them had entered the community for more than five years. Almost all of them told me they learned of lesbian identities such as *"lala"*, *"T"* and *"P"* from the Internet via message boards or chatrooms. Some of them were already having same-sex relationships before the advent of *tongzhi* cyber communities, while others only realized their sexuality or learned how to express it from the Internet. Informants usually searched keywords such as *"tongxinglian"* (homosexuality) or *"lesbian"* in English with local search engines. Searching *"tongxinglian"* in 2005, Chris (thirty years old), a Shanghai native, found a major *lala* website in China and the information of a *lala* bar in Shanghai. She then went to the bar and met a group of *lalas* there. At the time of our first interview in 2005, she had only come into touch with the local *lala* community for a month. Torn apart by the pressure to marry and by her same-sex desires, Chris was very troubled at that time. She was uncertain if it would be possible to have a future with a female lover. But after suffering intense marriage pressures for several years, she was determined to find a way out. When I returned to Shanghai a few months later, she happily introduced me to her first girlfriend, and was surrounded by a group of new *lala* friends. Two years later in 2007, Chris, by then going out with her second girlfriend, told me she was planning a cooperative marriage with a gay man. Chris's experience is illustrative of how the *tongzhi* cyber public can both inform and transform one's private life. Before Chris's entry into the cyber *lala* community, she could not even imagine a life with a same-sex lover. In 2005 when we first met, it had never occurred to her that she would one day have a cooperative marriage with a gay man, whom she would find on the Internet. Chris's life choices, in particularly those that unfolded over the years of study, have been greatly informed by the cyber public.

Chris's story shares a common element with those of many other informants. Many informants also began their "self"-searching journey on the Internet. Many of them, especially those born after the 1980s, had already known the terms for homosexuality such as *"tongxinglian"*, *"tongxingai"* (same-sex love), and *"tongzhi"* prior to their Internet searches—those terms having appeared more frequently in print and in public discussions during the reform period. Homosexuality has been popularly interpreted as a practice carried out by a distinctive group of people as defined and implied by experts in medical publications, legal discourse and academic studies. Therefore, although some of the informants did not consciously associate their homosexual practice or desires with a public homosexual identity, they were very often gradually called upon into this "self" revelation as soon as they launched Internet searches and began to engage in online interactions. Ying (in her early thirties) had a four-year same-sex relationship before she joined the cyber community in 2003. She was resistant to the idea of being a homosexual, and she disliked the term *tongxinglian*. Only after she found the online community did she start to associate herself with the identity category of *tongxinglian*,

> There were both male and female *tongzhi* in that chatroom. They were all quite young. When I first started to go to the chatroom, I just observed what was going on. I just checked out what they were talking about. Then I became surprised that there were so many people who shared similar experiences as me. I had never thought of that as being *tongxinglian*. At first, I tended to condemn them. I told myself I was different from them. But in reality, the more you read, the more verification you get, and you know you're one of them. Later, when I went to a voice chatroom as well as other websites, I kept finding things about them that resonated with me.[19]

Moon (twenty-two years old) recalled that she fell in love with a female classmate in university. Later, her classmate rejected her, declaring she was unable to return Moon's love as she was not a *tongxinglian*. It was only at that moment that Moon realized that others regarded her as a *tongxinglian*. She had never perceived herself in that way even though she admired women. Moon's girlfriend was particularly resistant to that socially stigmatized label. In 2003, out of curiosity and also a desire to understand herself more, Moon started to search for information on the Internet. She searched *"nütong"* (female *tongzhi*) on a local search engine,

> I typed in *"nütong"* on the Baidu search page, and a website and a few academic reports popped up. I did not choose to read the websites, but instead, I read the academic reports—just some writings by professors and mostly very scholarly writings. They discussed *"nütong"* very broadly, like how in the world of *"nütong"*, there are categories such as *"T"*, *"P"* and *"bufen"*. These concepts impressed upon my mind instantly, and I applied my relationship with [my girlfriend] to them. It also made these concepts clearer to me. Later, I browsed some of the websites. The first one I entered was called "When a dream begins". It's not a very sophisticated website, but it gathered a lot of *les*. So I read some of the writings on sex between *"nütong"*. That's where I got to know how women have sex with each other, like what oral sex is, or what to do with your fingers. I hadn't even known

about those basic things. Later I met a *nütong*, and she introduced me to a chatroom. She was the moderator of a women's website, and it was because of her that I entered into the chatroom. Once I got in, I was like—wow! All of the people here are *les*; there are so many of them. I'm not alone in this; I'm not a freak. In fact, there are so many people like myself![20]

The cyber public provided a framework for Moon to understand and articulate herself and her same-sex relationship. It initiated a process of self-discovery, and signalled a significant moment of self-empowerment and self-normalization. Moon has since then come to terms with her lesbian identity, and has started to understand her same-sex relationship in a new way. More importantly, the cyber encounters have allowed her to gain a positive understanding of homosexuality, while also introducing her to practical knowledge of having same-sex relationships.

Qing (twenty-seven years old) articulated very well how important the cyber community was to her,

My first thought was that: you think your own experience of being in love is unique, because it's very important to you. But once you go on the net and read many similar postings, and realize that having a crush on someone is something everyone goes through—like how hard it is to confess your feelings. Oh then you realize it's so common and popular! You find out that many people are like that on the net. That is to say, my first reaction was to say to myself: I'm not the only one, we're all united in this. Then the second was . . . They send out information about meet-ups or personal ads in search of partners. When you receive that sort of information, you feel it's normal for you to meet each other in person. Then you start to feel that they are no different from the people you see every day—they can lead good lives too. Then the third thing: when you talk about your shared ideas or the future, you start to feel . . . Like that time when I went to Beijing [and met some younger friends], it made me think if as teenagers they can live such lives, then my future can't be all that bad. They taught me hope. I wouldn't think of that in the past because I felt it was impractical; I couldn't see any examples or alternatives. But when I saw them, I saw the future.[21]

Apart from self-inauguration, the cyber community has allowed Qing to imagine a future together with a woman. The life experiences of other *lalas* circulating on the Internet are a powerful source of reference for the rest of the community. When many individuals are still exploring, or yet to explore, their desires; when many still fall short of imagining a way of life outside heterosexual marriage—the lived stories in the cyber public may help to forecast future blueprints for them.

The *tongzhi* cyber public has gradually extended to offline spaces. Salon meetings organized by local *lala* groups are held regularly in cities like Shanghai and Beijing. Participants come from different parts of the country. The meetings are always topical, covering issues related to *lalas*'s everyday life: coming out to parents, maintaining a relationship, and legal concerns for *tongzhi*. Salon meetings are another source of reference for women who want to pursue an alternative lifestyle. They present a physical space for the sharing and circulation of life stories that are otherwise unspoken and invisible in public life. They also cater to the needs of *lalas* who yearn for a safe, inclusive space to engage in face-to-face sharing and in-depth discussions.

Public Visibility and *Tongzhi* Existence

The increased public visibility of *tongzhi* in China in the past ten years is related to media interest of the subject. Early in the late 1990s, there were a handful of occasions of lesbians and gay men appearing on television programmes. Into the twenty-first century, more lesbians and gay men came out on television talk shows, newspapers, not to mention the cyberspace—as in the collective "coming out" of lesbians and gay men in the cyberspace since the late 1990s when the Internet opened to public use. Yet it is important to note that coming out in popular media and the Internet is attached with conditions. Those who can afford to appear in the public are usually required to be "model" homosexuals, who demonstrate qualities recognized by mainstream society. Those who can participate in collective cyber coming out are the technologically and culturally privileged. The conditions attached to coming out in public have contributed to the development of homonormative regulations (Duggan, 2003) that give preference to certain personal images, lifestyles, sexual practices, relationships and beliefs over the rest of the *tongzhi* community. It has also contributed to the question of *suzhi*—or qualities—in *tongzhi* communities in China, as critically examined by Lisa Rofel (2007) and Travis S. K. Kong (2011) in their studies of male *tongzhi* and "money boys". Also, the fast developing commercial *tongzhi* spaces serve only a limited segment of the *tongzhi* population. The internal exclusion or hierarchization of *tongzhi* communities will be discussed in Chapter 5.

The public discussions of homosexuality during the economic reform period have shaped the living context of *tongzhi* in China. Medical and legal understandings have dominated public knowledge of homosexuality. Discussions have long been confined to the domains of abnormal psychology and criminality. Even after homosexuality was removed from medical and criminal categories in 1997 and 2001 respectively, the image of homosexual people as perverts and potential criminals still persists in public imagination and in medical, legal and academic discourses as well. This has carried on until today. The circulation of knowledge about homosexuality and the appearance of *tongzhi* in the media vastly transform the public lives of *tongzhi*. In the private arena, one possible impact is that the increasing social awareness of homosexuality may make it more difficult for many closet *lalas* and gay men to cover up their sexuality or same-sex relationship in their families and marriages. For many of them in China, the only possible way to survive in day-to-day life would be to pass as heterosexuals.

In the following chapter, I will discuss the strategies *lala* women apply to cope with social demands in their private lives.

Chapter 3
Private Dilemma

When I open the closet, half of it has my clothes in it, the other half has hers. Every night, she lies next to me in bed. There is not one night when I am left alone. [*But the reality is*] I go on the net on my own. Whenever I am unhappy, I cry alone. I want my life to be infused with her presence. This home belongs to two people; it's not made up of only my stuff. I hope she can truly be a part of my life, completely and thoroughly. (Moon, in her early twenties)[1]

Beginning in the economic reform period, the country has seen significant changes concerning private life and sexual morality. Models of intimacy that deviated from the normative one (heterosexual monogamous marriage) began competing for legitimacy and acceptance. Alternative models such as singlehood, multiple partnership, cohabitation, extramarital relationship and same-sex relationship have entered public discussion relatively free from the ideological and moralistic constraints that typified the pre-reform era. However, the dominant position of heterosexual marriage as the only socially acceptable form of intimacy has not been threatened. One shared theme of informants' life narratives is the pressure of marriage. To almost all informants, married or unmarried, marriage is one major source of pressure in everyday life. The emergence of *tongzhi* communities since the late 1990s and the demand for exclusive same-sex relationship (that is not secondary to a heterosexual relationship) have put *tongzhi* in a difficult position to fulfil the obligation of marriage. In contemporary China, marriage is still assumed as an uncontested and a *natural* part of adult life. More than half of the key informants in this study were in their twenties at the time of interview, which is the so-called marriage age of women in China. This helps to explain why they considered the pressure of marriage as the major challenge in their life. It is important to note that the concerns of individual *tongzhi* in China vary by age, gender identification, class, ethnicity, religious belief, geographical location and the salient rural-urban divide. The problem of marriage as discussed in this chapter represents the most talked about challenge of *lalas* in Shanghai during the 2005–2011 period.

As direct state control of people's private lives through the *danwei* system or communal surveillance gradually retreated in urban China during the economic reform period, the family has become the most effective institution in monitoring individuals' sexualities in the everyday context. In this chapter, I will discuss the dilemma *lala* women are facing in their private lives regarding marriage and their same-sex sexualities. I will look at how *lalas* are symbolically neglected in public discussion about *tongzhi* and dismissed from being autonomous sexual subjects in both public and private domains. I will focus particularly on forms of social control imposed by the institutions of marriage and family on *lalas*' everyday life, and the deep-rooted stigma attached to female celibacy in China.

The Pressure of Marriage

Informants suffered most from the conflicts between family expectations and their same-sex relationships. While encouraged and empowered by the recently formed *tongzhi* communities to imagine and pursue a life that can realize same-sex desires, their heterosexual families are demanding them to keep their same-sex desires and relationships in the closet—at least not to display them in the family space. Such a compulsory demand has forced many informants to pass as heterosexuals in their families. Their heterosexual acting includes self-monitoring of gender expression (especially for informants who identify as Ts), hiding any signs of their sexualities and involvement in *lala* communities in daily interactions, attending blind dates arranged by parents and relatives, or having cooperative marriages. Straight performance allows *lalas* to survive in the heteronormative family space, while at the same time, it has an effect of reinforcing the boundary of normality and deviance. In the following part, I will discuss how important marriage is in contemporary urban China and how the family has become increasingly crucial as a gatekeeper of the heterosexual institution.

Heterosexual monogamous marriage has been the state-enforced model of intimate union since the introduction of the country's first Marriage Law in 1950. It is supported by and is closely aligned with other state policies of resource allocation, social status, and communal control. It has long been upheld by the medical institution as the most biologically desirable and "normal" form of sexual and psychological relationship. Experts from different authoritative domains such as legal, medical and official women's and youth groups have been cooperating with each other for decades to promote the model as the only legitimate, healthy and morally correct form of adult intimate activity. The state-enforced naturalization of the monogamous heterosexual marriage has led to a discursive erasure of other forms of intimate relationship and sexual subject positions. People who do not fit into the dominant model can only live as sexual deviants, or as inferior citizens with a lesser share of resources and social respect. For women, the dominant heterosexual marriage model ascribes to them the social roles of wife and mother. Adult women are demanded to perform these two roles when they reach the suitable age for marriage.[2] Marriage has remained a very secure and powerful institution even after the reform period. According to the official data collected in 2004, 19.5% of the entire population aged 15 or over was unmarried (that is, never married). Unmarried females constituted 16.5% of the entire female population aged 15 or over; unmarried males constituted 22.5% of the entire male population aged 15 or over (China Statistics Press 2005). The 2004 data indicated no significant change in the size of unmarried population aged 15 or above over the previous five years (1999–2004) in China. In 1999, 18.8% of the entire population aged 15 or over was unmarried—the gender-specific figures being 15.3% for females, and 22.2% for males (China Statistics Press 2000).[3] The figures of 2004 also showed a drastic decline of unmarried populations in the age categories of 20–24, 25–29, and 30–34, which are 69.3%, 21.4% and 5.7% respectively (China Statistic Press 2005). The numbers indicated that the norms surrounding a suitable age for marriage still had a tight grip on most people in China. In urban China, ages 25 to 29 are considered the most suitable ages for marriage for both sexes. By that age, many will have finished their education, and probably have a stable job. Most people will experience the strongest and also the most organized pressure of marriage during these few years before they turn thirty. Parents, relatives, or even colleagues and friends will start to introduce prospective mates to them and arrange meetings. Even in Shanghai, a city which is generally considered to be non-traditional in many social aspects, marriage remains a normative lifestyle for most people. The percentage of unmarried population of the city in 2004 (18.2%) was even slightly lower than that of the whole country (China Statistic Press 2005).

The pressure to marry is particularly felt by women. As my informant Tan (in her mid-twenties) said, the pressure usually comes earlier for women. The pressure of marriage can come as early as in someone's early twenties around the time when she finishes her education, and reach a climax when she approaches mid-twenties. Tan's assessment may seem to contradict Lisa Rofel's early observation of the Beijing gay scene that says women face less pressure of marriage (Rofel 1997). In reality, both gender groups may suffer from the pressure of marriage, but this pressure may be experienced in different ways. Women not only have to face the pressure at an earlier age, but they are also less capable of escaping it because women's freedom of mobility is still more limited than that of men in China. Their freedom to move out of their parents' home before marriage or to relocate to another city is relatively restricted. This is particularly the case for women from major urban centres such as Shanghai. They have even fewer reasons to convince their families to let them relocate to other parts of the country, compared with women from rural or less developed areas. Economic inferiority is another factor that puts many women in a disadvantaged situation under the marriage pressure. The ever-widening gender income gap in capitalized China indicates a diminishing economic possibility for women to have a financially independent life outside of marriage. In this manner, marriage becomes a practical way for the disadvantaged group to attain upward social mobility.

The punitive effects are obvious for people in China who choose not to marry. Even though direct state control over private lives has weakened, the *danwei* system, which has been in place for decades, still exerts its control on various aspects of people's lives. Married people in state-run or affiliated enterprises receive more economic and other forms of material rewards than unmarried people. For example, married people are assigned bigger apartments while unmarried people may have to wait for years before they can get an independent housing unit. Fang Gang (2005), in his qualitative study of women and men with multiple sex partners in China, found that people within the job reassignment system tend to worry more about the exposure of their sexual behaviour at work than people with jobs from the private sector. Although the economic grip of *danwei* on people's daily lives has lessened after the reform period, its political and moral surveillance still constitutes a source of stress for people with socially disapproved sexual behaviour.

Besides economic benefits, married people enjoy a much higher social status. Marriage in China is understood as a rite of passage to adulthood. One cannot be socially recognized as an adult until s/he has her/his own conjugal family. This cultural belief is expressed through the association of marriage with social responsibility. To be an adult means taking up more social responsibilities and being a productive citizen to the country. This means a citizen's social responsibility is to get married and to reproduce the next generation. In other words, if a person has reached the age of marriage but does not get married, s/he will be regarded as avoiding the responsibility s/he needs to fulfil to family and society, and hence s/he cannot be considered as a responsible adult. Marriage is also connected with one's psychological, biological and moral wellness. To lead a "normal" life is not so much a personal choice, but a matter of social survival of the person concerned and her/his family as well.

The Demand of a "Normal" Life

The social expectation to lead a "normal" life is highly valued in China. The force of social conformity is evident from daily language usage—such as the choice of many informants to use "normal" or "not normal" to judge different kinds of lifestyle or sexuality and life choices such as marriage and childbearing. Almost all informants have experienced the pressure of marriage. Most of them have attended matchmaking meetings arranged by parents, relatives, colleagues or friends. It seems that most of them accepted that marriage is not something one can take full control of. They understood it more as fulfilling a responsibility to parents and to society. In her mid-twenties and not yet married, Shu expressed a view on marriage quite representative of women in her age group,

> Since marriage is not a simple matter of love, you need to consider many things, such as family [and] society . . . A person's marital status can affect society, and a marriage can therefore affect things that one might not have thought would matter before. It can also well provide grounds for someone to attack you. And this will make your parents worry.[4]

Informants always emphasized their duty to their parents when talking about marriage. Especially for married informants, marriage is understood as an individual's duty to satisfy her/his family's expectation and to not upset the social order. Ying had met her first girlfriend before her wedding, and since then, she had been having a difficult long-term extramarital relationship. But she had never thought of not getting married,

> I had never thought of marriage as optional. I felt that everyone must get married . . . I didn't have any point of reference. I felt that everyone had to walk this path. Maybe at that time I thought I was just a bit different from others. But still you cannot upset the normal social order just because you're different or special. You still have to bear responsibilities for your family, for your parents. I didn't see how I could have the ability to challenge [all this]. At that time, both of us (Ying and her girlfriend) never thought about [not getting married]. It didn't seem like an issue. It didn't feel like a question worth serious consideration because it's simply unimaginable to consider its possibility.[5]

Apart from responsibility, Ying also mentioned the importance of having role models. Although she knew there are women who never marry, she had never encountered any positive role models. Similarly, she did not have any idea of what a lesbian's life would be like when she started her first same-sex relationship. Ying was uncertain if it would be possible to not get married and to start a family with a woman:

> At that time, it was really terrifying to hear people mentioning those three words (*tongxinglian*). When our friends made fun of us and said, "you two look like you're *tongxinglian*", my girlfriend and I would fight back at once. At first it was about not being able to come to terms with your own being. But now I understand the reason we fought back was also because we did

not acknowledge our own behaviour . . . Neither of us knew what to do at that time when we got together. We would always cry when we called each other, and talk about what we should do, because there was nothing to refer to. I think if we had had access to the Internet at that time, we might have gotten together; we might have stayed together and overcome many obstacles. You basically won't think of living this kind of life. You feel there is no future for this. You think that no one would embark on this road or that this road is impossible to begin with. You feel that everyone should get married . . . I remember the night before my wedding, [my girlfriend] went with me and stayed at a hotel. There were many relatives at my home, and it gave me an excuse to stay out in order to get a good rest. So she stayed with me at a hotel room. The next morning, I had to return home to put my makeup on and to prepare for the wedding. It was really . . . together we were crying and crying till four in the morning. That was the night before my wedding.[6]

Ying repeatedly mentioned that it had never occurred to her when she was younger that she could have an alternative way of life other than marriage. Marriage to her is not a choice but a natural process of life.

Coral (in her mid-thirties) was married, and had a stable *lala* relationship. To her, marriage is a duty and a collective matter,

If you have never gotten married, you probably won't know what it feels like to have the weight of marriage on your shoulders, or what it really means. If I put it simply as responsibility, you might wonder what it means by responsibility. You might feel it's an abstract idea. But actually, marriage is not just between two persons; it involves a lot more people, way more than the two persons. You're talking about families, even friends, colleagues. You won't understand—as a person who hasn't gotten married before, you won't really understand it. You might be able to understand my reasoning, or sympathize with me. But there are other feelings that you have no idea of.[7]

For women, marriage is also an economic decision. In general, women are expected to marry men who are economically better off. It is materially beneficial for a woman to get married in China. For instance, the contemporary marriage custom in Shanghai requires the male's side of the family to provide housing for the new couple. Housing is always the biggest economic investment in a marriage. There is a popular saying in Shanghai which says: Having a daughter now is much better than having a son since the investment in a son for his marriage is far more than that for a daughter. Women may experience the pressure of marriage for material reasons. For economically dependent *lalas*, it is harder to convince their families that they can support themselves without marrying a man who is economically better off. In my research, it is evident that women who have decided not to get married often rate the importance of economic self-sufficiency very highly. I will elaborate more on this factor in the next chapter.

"Abnormal" Women

There is a history of stigmatizing women who depart from the state-enforced heterosexual monogamous model in China. The category of "abnormal" women consists of unmarried women, impotent women, sexually promiscuous women, asexual women, homosexual women, and sexually dominating women. Women who deviate from the dominant model will not only be punished in formal or informal ways, but they will also be categorized as sexual deviants and considered a threat to social order and morality. A hierarchy of stigmatization exists for "abnormal" women. In contemporary urban China, the least stigmatized categories are unmarried women and impotent women, followed by sexually active or promiscuous heterosexual women. Homosexual women remain the most socially unrecognized sexual "deviants". Unlike sexually active heterosexual women, women with same-sex sexual practices are more often dismissed by society. Their sexuality is unthinkable in the dominant heterosexual model of an active male and a passive female. Li Yinhe (2002a), in her work on male homosexuality in China, states that since same-sex sexual activity does not associate itself with marriage and reproduction, it is considered both "improper" and "insignificant" in China (p. 254). Women's same-sex sexuality, as it is unimaginable in the heterosexual model, is even more marginalized. Female homosexuality is still considered not normal in popular imagination: it may be much less severely regulated and punished by the legal institution as their male counterparts, but the cultural dismissal of them is as forcible as other more visible forms of punishment.

To lessen the stigmatizing effect of being an unmarried and a homosexual woman at the same time, many of the younger informants resorted to telling their parents they want to stay single for life. Although staying single is not a preferable and socially recognized lifestyle, it is easier for parents to comprehend it than homosexuality. However, prejudice against single women is still widely present in society. In early years before the reform period, *daling qingnian* (overage young people) was regarded as a social problem. For overage unmarried women, the term *lao gu'niang* (old girl) is still popularly used in Shanghai. *Lao gu'niang* is usually associated with physical unattractiveness, poor interpersonal relationships, poor health, and personality defects. The status of marriage is therefore understood as closely associated with one's "internal essence". By extension, parents will also be affected and stigmatized if they have an unmarried and "overage" daughter.

Chris thought about staying single after a frustrating experience with dating a man for one year (to please her parents). But she knew her parents would never understand or allow her to be celibate, and therefore, she decided not to tell them if she really opted for such a life. Her colleagues reacted negatively when she once mentioned to them her plan to stay single,

> I'm not going to hurt others, but I also don't want myself to get hurt. This is why even if I'm unable to find a loving relationship, I wouldn't mind—I'd rather be single. Yet this creates more pressure for me, because it is harder for families and friends to accept my decision. They think that in any case I should get married, be settled, and have a family. I told them that I am not suitable for this kind of life because I prefer freedom and don't want to be restrained in any form. I have told them before. Of course I did not tell my parents that I wanted to be single. I think there's no way they would accept it. I told my colleagues and friends that I wanted to be single, and they were so shocked! They said, "How can you!" and immediately told me not to think this way.[8]

The popular understanding of single women is still dominated by negative stereotypes. To many, staying single for life means leading a miserable and incomplete life, and subjecting oneself and one's family to communal surveillance (usually in the form of gossips) if she is an overage single woman. Since marriage is the one and only imaginable and socially approved way of life, any other alternative life choices will be inevitably subjected to social scrutiny. The family of the single woman and herself will attract much unwanted attention directed towards the woman's private life. What is actually implied by seemingly well-intended enquiries is the questioning of the woman's physical or psychological well-being. Ling (twenty-seven years old), who had just officially registered for marriage with a gay man to form a cooperative marriage at the time of our interview in 2007, explained very well the reason why parents are so frustrated if their daughter chooses to stay single, and why people presume the right to interfere with the private life of a single woman,

> A single woman usually gives others the impression of being unfortunate. Why? Who cares if she's a career woman? You would still think that her love life is less than perfect. If not for the simple reason of not having a man who loves her—or even, not having a woman who loves her—then she would never choose to spend life alone. She is single because she cannot find a wonderful and harmonious relationship, one that satisfies her needs. Why would she be single if she can have a good relationship? It doesn't matter if she's career-driven. Even a workaholic won't be like that. It is still the power of social pressure. Parents would feel that their child is by herself, and other outsiders would come up with different sorts of reasons—and then the pressure becomes too much to bear . . . Also, on many occasions you become the target of much concern if you aren't married. Someone might say to you, is your daughter still unmarried, or, does she have a boyfriend? Or something like that. If you're not married, you'll always be the target of this kind of concern. Once you're married, people leave you alone.[9]

However, there are parents of informants who would rather have their daughters remain single than to have a homosexual relationship. It might be relatively easier for parents to integrate an unmarried daughter into the heterosexual kinship system. A celibate life does not challenge the core values of heteronormativity, while homosexuality is an unambiguous departure from the norm, violently disturbing the entire heterosexual framework of marriage and reproduction. A few informants thus chose to come out to their parents in a gradual and non-confrontational way as opting for a life without marriage.

Family and Marriage

With the power of political intervention fading out from people's everyday life, contemporary Chinese parents, who have grown up in a uniform society in which any politically or socially deviant behaviours would affect their livelihood severely, are now actively taking up the role as guards to ensure that their children are leading a normative heterosexual life and are not becoming deviants in any sense. Even though there is a growing population of younger urban dwellers who choose to remain single, to the parents of most of my informants, a life without marriage is unthinkable. These parents believe that responsible parents should help their children find a good marital partner and to start a new family.[10] They are eagerly involved in the matchmaking of their children, having committed both emotional and economic investments in their children's marriage.

Parents play a significant role in their daughters' decisions around marriage, including the decision to get married or to remain single, when to get married and the choice of spouse. Relatives are the second most powerful group in deciding the marriage partner of younger family members. Although strictly arranged marriages are very rare in urban areas like Shanghai, semi-arranged marriages are not uncommon. Meetings with potential partners introduced by relatives or friends of parents are usually arranged for younger members in a family who have reached the suitable age for marriage. After the initial meeting, the young people can decide whether or not they want to proceed and develop the relationship. According to a survey done by Li Yinhe (2002b) on marriage choices among women and men in China, 40% of the two hundred respondents had their marriage primarily decided by themselves but with the approval of parents; 13% had their marriage primarily decided by parents but with their own approval. Only 17% managed to be in full control of their marriage, despite the fact that 55% of all respondents said they would prefer to have full control over their marriage.

As discussed above, an unmarried homosexual woman is doubly stigmatized and marginalized by the normative heterosexual discourse. There is a hierarchy of social recognition concerning one's marital status in China; in decreasing order, this is: married, single, divorced. Being a homosexual person bears greater stigma than being single or divorced. In recent years, in the context of increasing public discussion about homosexuality in the country, a few parents have come out to the media to support their gay son or lesbian daughter. An Internet survey done by a website in China found that over 70% of respondents (3,977 in total) said s/he would be able to accept if her/his child is a homosexual (quoted from www.cctv.com, 6 November 2007). The survey was conducted immediately after the airing of reports about Wu Youjian, a mother in Guangzhou who publicly supported her gay son on the media. The decision of Wu was applauded by many on the Internet as a brave act by a supportive mother. This partly explains why the survey results were extraordinarily positive. Contrary to the findings of the survey, most of my informants did not receive any support from their parents concerning their sexuality. Some of them have never thought about the possibility of obtaining their parents' support. Jenny (in her mid-twenties) said her mother had once said to her, "I would rather you don't get married for the rest of your life. I will not give you my approval in this kind of matter (being a homosexual)." As previously mentioned, the cultural belief in China states that a person can only be recognized as a fully developed adult when s/he gets married and has her/ his own nuclear family. Staying single means that one does not have the social status of being an autonomous adult. For this reason, parents, relatives or even friends feel obliged to persuade the single daughter in the family to find a mate. It is not honourable to the family if they have an overage unmarried daughter. Tan (twenty-seven years old) concluded that it is all about the *mianzi* (face) of parents,

> It is because [parents] feel they have no "face". You are no longer a part of the family once you get married and you won't be cared for so much. It's like taking care of their "face".[11]

Usually marriage and work (or study) are the two reasons which allow women to live away from their parental homes in China. For many, finding work in another city is not a likely option; therefore, marriage is the only reason left for one to leave her parents. This reflects the tighter familial control parents in China have over daughters. Men enjoy a much higher degree of freedom concerning the choice of abode and mobility in general. It is unimaginable to many parents to have an unmarried daughter living away from them for reasons other than "proper" ones like work and study. It is especially hard for informants to move out and live alone or with their partner when their natal families dwell in the same city. The problem is compounded by the fact that many of my informants—those born after the 1980s—were first-generation children under the single child policy in China. As a woman and the only child in the family, it is extremely difficult for them to move out before marriage.

Chris is a typical case. She was a Shanghai native and a single child who lived with her parents. She was aware of the difficulty of getting rid of her parents' control over her. However, it was impossible for her to leave Shanghai to work in another city in China. Shanghai is already one of the most developed cities in the country. Unlike her *lala* friends from other less developed parts of the country, Chris could not use the same excuse of leaving her hometown for better career development and life. She could only resort to another economic incentive to convince her parents of her plan to move out,

> The only way I can leave my family completely is to move out and buy a flat for myself. My parents definitely won't let me rent a flat and move out. But if I bought a flat then they can say nothing. Putting these two pressures together—if my family didn't pressurize me, then my desire to buy a flat would not be that strong. Of course, I'll still feel pressurized because I can't keep renting a flat for me and [my girlfriend]. I will feel insecure. I have to buy a flat. But with family pressure I've shortened the timeframe within which I plan to buy a flat. It could've been longer, like five or ten years' time.[12]

It is quite common for *lalas* to refer to economic or material recognition whenever they talk about how to come out to their parents or how to persuade them of their choice to stay single. Since economic success is highly regarded in the Chinese family, a higher economic status can "compensate" for a marginalized positioning caused by a socially stigmatized sexual status. This explains why *lalas* in China heavily emphasize material security and success, as well as being able to live life as well as (if not better than) married women. Material recognition is used to compensate for their lack of recognition in the sexual aspect. And to many, it is a way not only to free themselves from familial control, but also to make up for their parents' loss, for having deprived them of a "normal" family life with grandchildren and sons-in-law surrounding them. I term this kind of compensation tactic as the "politics of public correctness". It represents a logic in which one tries to outperform in other aspects of life to achieve the familial and social recognition needed to compensate for her sexual abnormality, so that in the end, her sexuality is accepted and traded off with other public goods. The politics of public correctness will be further discussed in Chapter 5.

Familial control of homosexuality can also be found in the policing of the daughter's gender expression. It is obvious in the lives of informants who have a masculine or androgynous gender expression. May's (in her mid-twenties) experience gives a typical demonstration of a parent's anxiety over gender abnormality and the implied association of masculine or androgynous gender expression with lesbianism,

> If I don't have a boyfriend or I look androgynous, [May's mother] will raise her suspicions or even ask me directly if I am [a homosexual]. (Interviewer: *Has she asked before?*) Yes, she has, but I did not answer her directly. She did not pursue the question any further. Sometimes people have a certain

degree of sensitivity; you can't push on certain matters. (*Have you always been androgynous since you were young?*) Yes, but sometimes I appear more feminine as well, rather than being a pure *T* or a pure *P*. I'm more like *bufen*.[13] (*But your mother is still suspicious?*) A little bit. But in the last two years, I've tried to appear more feminine by wearing dresses and growing out my hair. I took some photos for her as evidence. [Laughs.] (*She is more at ease now?*) Yes. It's obvious that she feels more comforted, because she has a very emotional and childish side. You can tell right away she's unhappy if for a day I wear a shirt or cut my hair short. But if she sees me the next day with a skirt on, growing out my hair, wearing heels, standing up straight, walking with my head held high, she will be ecstatic. She will feel that it's more normal this way and think the other day was just an aberration. [Laughs.][14]

Parental gender policing ensures that no sign of homosexuality is exposed in the family space. Consistent regulation requires the family member concerned to put on a heterosexual guise whenever she appears in the family setting. Without being seen or heard, there is neither discursive nor physical space for *lalas* to present themselves in their heterosexual families as a fully recognized homosexual subject. From Ling's experience, we see that she was rendered invisible as a homosexual subject. Her partner's mother referred to Ling as a relative. Ling recounted,

There's no way I can join all [my partner's] family activities. I can eat and sleep over at her place. I can spend time with her, watch television and hang out. But that's it. I cannot take part in public activities. That's impossible. If her mother's friends are there, she'll say I'm her sister's daughter, her niece or something like that to cover up for me. I cannot isolate myself from her home—definitely not. I'm often at her place and people often see me around. It's not easy at all.[15]

Ling's partner was living with her parents. Ling was allowed to have dinner and to stay overnight in her partner's home. But while she was welcomed in the private home, she was prohibited from any family activities in public that involved other kin and family friends. The boundary of the public/the private, or the inside/the outside, is clearly defined in Ling's case. In the context of the family, non-heterosexual subjects are confined to the invisible, behind closed doors where homosexuality is tolerated. When a homosexual subject is exposed in the public, she will be disguised as a heterosexual family member. The refusal of her partner's mother to acknowledge Ling publicly is one instance illustrating how *lalas* are symbolically eliminated from the heterosexual family, and how *lala* relationship and *lala* subjects can only have a closeted existence in the family space.

Private Dilemma

Lalas face conflicting expectations from their families and their *tongzhi* identification. The conflicts are most pronounced in the pressure of marriage. The
heterosexual monogamous model has long been naturalized by state institutions and social customs as the only biologically healthy and socially acceptable form of intimate relationship. Other forms of sexual practices, either
non-heterosexual or non-monogamous, are denied the status of proper or
normal. Women in their twenties, which constituted the major age group in this
study, face the most intense forms of marriage pressure from parents, relatives
and even other secondary social networks. *Lalas* are doubly marginalized by
society for their gender and sexuality. As women, they are not culturally recognized as autonomous sexual subjects, unless represented as sexual deviants
or as "abnormal" sexually active women. As *tongzhi*, their same-sex desires
and relationships are frequently trivialized, and are not regarded as anything
"real" or substantial. Unlike men, women are discursively considered as sexual
non-subjects. Their intimate same-sex relationships are usually disregarded
by society. *Lalas* are considered less a threat to the heterosexual order, and are
generally more "tolerated" in Chinese families. However, tolerance cannot be
equated with recognition or acceptance. In many cases, lesbianism is tolerated
because of general ignorance regarding same-sex sexuality between women. It
is precisely the double non-recognition of *lalas* as sexual subjects and women
as autonomous sexual beings that has led to their discursive erasure from both
public and private domains.

Chapter 4
Negotiating the Public and the Private

> It's like being pulled by two different forces—non-stop. It's just like that, and it's never-ending. (Ying, in her early thirties)[1]

It is one of the central concerns of this book to document and examine *lala* women's everyday struggles and strategies in post-reform China. The pressure of marriage, whether it is the pressure to get married or to maintain a marriage, is shared by almost every *lala* women I met in Shanghai and other cities such as Beijing and Guangzhou. As discussed in the last chapter, the fact that marriage was cited as the major source of pressure in daily life is because most of the informants in this study were in their twenties at the time of interview (the years 2005–11). They were also the dominant group in local *lala* communities in Shanghai and other cities at that time. Women in China in their early to late twenties are expected to get married. The concerns expressed by informants are reflective of their age, gender and geographical location. For informants, the conflicts were mainly expressed through familial control and the pressure to get married. To endure such conflicts, most of them found themselves seeking solutions in two directions. Some struggled to align themselves with heterosexual norms. Others explored ways to avoid direct confrontation with their families, be they their natal or conjugal families. The heterosexual institution is safeguarded by discourses of familial harmony and collective responsibility. The emphasis on familial harmony in Chinese families is particularly forceful in regulating informants' relationships with parents and husbands. It is also the major cause pushing some into a self-imposed isolation from their family and heterosexual marriage. For others, it has pushed them into an extreme form of heterosexual acting: the cooperative marriage (*hezuo hunyin*, or *xingshi hunyin*), a new form of intimate union and family formed by *lalas* and gay men under the pressure of marriage. In this chapter, I will discuss the various ways *lalas* use to cope with the pressure from family and marriage in their everyday life. The first part focuses on the interactions between *lalas* and their natal family. The second part examines the situation of married *lalas* in greater detail.

Coping with Family

Most informants felt that the biggest pressure of marriage came from their parents. Some may have also experienced similar pressure from friends or cow-orkers, but it was usually easier for them to dismiss comments from secondary social groups that were more detached from their immediate everyday life. The heavy emotional attachment and responsibility towards their parents that informants imposed on themselves were the major cause of their frustration and guilt over their same-sex sexuality. Siblings seemed neither a significant source of pressure nor support to informants. Informants with siblings usually chose not to tell them about their sexuality. For informants who were the only child, we cannot assume that in all cases they faced more pressure from their parents. This depended on their relationship with their parents, and whether they lived with or away from their parents. It is crucial to consider the changing power dynamics between Chinese parents and the single child, and what impact this has on the lives of *tongzhi* in family and society. With a growing *tongzhi* population in China who are from the single-child generation, it is hoped that more studies will be carried out to examine the specific challenges and experiences concerning this internally diverse group.

In and out of the closet

The biggest struggle for informants was how to reveal to their parents their sexuality and same-sex relationship, and whether they should let them know at all. In China, the act or process of revealing to others one's sexual orientation is called *"chugui"* (getting out of the closet). As indicated by the frequency of discussion in cyber forums and offline salon meetings, *chugui* is the topic that is most talked about and which generates the greatest concern in Shanghai's *lala* communities. Many discussions are centred on the decision of *chugui*—whether one should come out to parents and other acquaintances, the strategic planning of *chugui*, and its possible consequences. Local *lala* communities hold different views about *chugui*. *Chugui* is usually understood not as a single verbal act, but as an extended process involving long-term effort and careful planning. Most informants did not agree with an impulsive act of *chugui* to parents, cowork-ers or straight friends. As most informants were past their mid-twenties and many were financially competent working women, the social and professional risks involved in *chugui* were relatively higher for them than for the younger generation. Their cautious attitude is representative of the views of the more mature group in the community. May, an experienced *lala* hotline counsellor in Shanghai, was sceptical about the necessity to *chugui*,

Although coming out is a very admirable behaviour, it also depends on the situation. It's not like you are going to be a martyr. (Interviewer: *Will you say so when you are on the hotline?*) Yes, I tell callers that I do not encourage one to come out. This is a very serious matter, one that requires serious consideration, especially if your conditions don't allow you to come out. It's about being realistic. I often tell them directly in a stark, naked way, can *you* (said in a prolonged tone) afford to come out?[2]

Many discussed coming out in the context of material reality. They believed that the process would be smoother if one is able to prove to her parents she is financially capable. And to some, coming out is evidently not at all an option.

Younger informants tended to be more active in confessing their sexual orientation to parents. Ya, who was in her early twenties, initiated the topic with her parents. They finally accepted her same-sex relationship after a period of non-communication, during which Ya moved out to stay with her girlfriend in a rented apartment. Bai, also in her early twenties, told her mother directly about her desire for women. Fortunately, her mother supported her, and even came out publicly as a parent of a *lala* daughter. In 2005, her mother appeared publicly as a guest speaker in a class on homosexuality studies at Fudan University in Shanghai. Another younger informant, Moon, confessed to her mother by making use of the countrywide craze over the "Super Girls" Singing Contest (*chaoji nüsheng*),[3]

My mum also likes both of them (the two "Super Girls" finalists), and she knows of the rumours about them being a couple, too. I also told her. Other entertainment news also reported that Li Yuchun kissed some girls—this and that. My mum saw some of the photos, too. My mum has always liked her. Then I suddenly felt it was the right timing. My mum knew so much about Li Yuchun and He Jie as homosexuals, especially Li Yuchun. All these negative coverage did not make my mum like her less. Instead, she introduced her to all her friends and colleagues so that they could also follow her. There was this time when she was watching the finals of "Super Girls", all nervous, happy and terribly excited at the same time, I asked her directly, "Mum, why do you like Li Yuchun?" Then she went on and on about how much she liked her, and about how when Li Yuchun cried she would also cry with her and all that. I went on asking, "Did you know that Li Yuchun likes girls?" "It doesn't matter. She's so boyish—I've already thought of that." Then I said, "Do you believe that she liked me before?" My mum looked at me and said, "You two went to the same university and were in the same year? No way." "I rejected her." My mom then asked sadly, "Why did you reject her?" I just smiled and said, "You go back to watching television." . . . I went on to say that there are plenty of girls like Li Yuchun in every city, every country, and throughout the world, but that a lot of people don't get it. I said there are tens of millions in China, many in the city where I lived, and that there are even more in my university.[4]

Moon continued the conversation with a hearty confession to her mother. It was a successful *chugui*. She was received positively by her mother.

There were a few informants whose parents found out their sexualities by accident. Jenny (in her mid-twenties) was one of them. Her parents chose to avoid the topic altogether after many bitter confrontations. It is quite common for parents to turn to a "don't ask, don't tell" approach when signs of their daughter's homosexuality surface. Chris's parents had been suspicious of her sexuality for some time, but they never spoke about it or asked her directly. Instead, they reverted to a tactic of actively arranging matchmaking meetings for Chris. At the time, Chris was approaching thirty.

For others who could not come out directly to their parents, they usually adopted the following two approaches. One was "to come out 'softly' and gradually", in what some have termed as the strategy of *ruan chugui* ("'soft' coming out"). Flora,[5] a Shanghai native in her late twenties, strategized her coming out by first showing a picture of her and her girlfriend to her parents casually, and then occasionally inviting her girlfriend over for dinner with her parents. She wanted to prepare her parents for the fact that sooner or later, she would move out with her girlfriend and would come out about their relationship. Another popular coping strategy with parents was to not tell them at all. The principles of filial piety and familial harmony govern the decision to *chugui* to parents. Many of my informants chose to leave home for another city after they decided to pursue a life that is contrary to their parents' expectation. Ying, a married woman in her early thirties, decided to leave her parents and her husband after a traumatic breakup with her second girlfriend. When I met her in Shanghai, Ying was studying in a local university. She had had a serious health crisis the year before she left her hometown. She recounted in detail a defining scene when she was staying and being taken care of at her parents' home,

> I felt bad looking at my parents. I remember vividly this one time when I stayed at their place for a week because I was sick. Each time before a meal, they would push open the door slightly to check if I was sleeping. They would always ask me what I wanted to eat. It was hard on me. I didn't feel like eating, but I pretended to. It became too hard on me afterwards. It was also too much for them physically and emotionally to look after me. Then one afternoon, I got up from the bed suddenly and told them I wanted to go home. In fact, my body was too weak. My parents tried to stop me. November is usually very cold back in the North. I hadn't brought any warm clothes when I first returned home. But I put on my coat and told them I was going home, without discussing with them. I didn't listen to them either. I put on my coat, opened the door to my room, and left. My mother kept saying out loud, "You can't go back. There's no one to take care of you." But she saw how adamant I was about leaving, so she went back into the house to fetch my jacket. I didn't know this. I had already rushed out, caught a taxi and gotten inside. I was running so fast that I didn't notice

the cold wind. When I turned around to look, I saw my mother holding my jacket and running after me. I'll never forget this picture for the rest of my life. This is why I thought if I chose to live this kind of life, I could never do it in front of them . . . I might never come out on my own. It's not because I don't want to face it. I feel that if by doing so you hurt people around you whom you love, then better not. Avoid it while you can, right? It doesn't matter with others, but with your parents . . . you can never leave them behind just for your own sake. I've already done this before. I'll certainly try to avoid that from now on.[6]

The feelings of guilt and being an unfilial daughter put many informants in long-term suffering, and prompted some to leave their natal families. Huang,[7] in her late twenties, literally fled to Shanghai to avoid a marriage arranged by her parents in her small hometown. Qi, also in her late twenties, came to Shanghai for a more anonymous social life, one which would be impossible in the small town where she grew up. She described her hometown as a place where one's whereabouts is closely monitored by people on the streets, as social networks are so tightly intertwined that all residents are connected in one way or another. Jenny, a Shanghai native, was planning to leave China with her girlfriend. To her, it was the fear of losing face that led her parents to react strongly to her same-sex relationship,

Actually, parents always want you to be happy. I feel that the problem is more about their "face". We have many relatives and friends here [in Shanghai]. That's why I thought it might be good if I left the country. They can tell others that I'm out of the country and I don't want to get married. They cannot see you, so even if you come out to them, there's no need for them to tell others. Just like that time when my father said to me, "You can't be like this in China." He just said this to me. "China is not that open yet. If you keep to your ways . . . you cannot raise your head at work or anywhere."[8]

If Jenny lives outside China, her parents will have an excuse to explain why their daughter is not married. The physical distance will relieve both parties from the pressure created by Jenny's sexuality and her singleness. Matty, a Shanghai native in her mid-twenties, had also decided to leave China. She had kept her three-year relationship in complete secrecy from family and co-workers. Although she lived an affluent life in Shanghai, she had decided to start a new but probably much less comfortable life in a foreign country with her girlfriend. Matty considered leaving China as the only option left to her,

Although some would say that love between two persons has nothing to do with others, at least we shouldn't put pressure on the people around us or affect them. You shouldn't let what you do affect other people's lives negatively . . . I feel that they just don't know how to process [the situation]. If you can leave your family out of it, just leave them out. You know you'll

get yelled at if you talk about it, so there's no point. Wait until the day when
you have no choice but to bring up the matter. Hide it at least for now. Don't
talk about it. It won't do you any good . . ."[9]

Coming out was not a viable option to many informants. Many *lalas* adopted
the spatial strategy of leaving one's hometown and immediate social networks,
especially as mobility within and even outside the country is greatly enhanced
after the reform period. The opening up of geographical space through the
economy's marketization indeed allowed a number of *lalas* to break away from
familial control and intense social surveillance. But moving between cities
or even between countries is not an option available to everyone. Mobility is
highly restricted by cultural and economic capital. It is especially hard for out-
siders to survive in Shanghai, a city with an ever-rising cost of living.

As discussed in the previous chapter, some informants would tell their
parents about their desire to lead a celibate life in order to avoid marital pressure
and to prevent a direct confrontation. Although a life without marriage is still
considered as less preferable to the older generations, it carries much less
stigma as compared to homosexuality. For economically well-off *lalas*, it serves
as a convenient justification for their choice to stay unmarried. Liu, a Shanghai
native in her early thirties, had a well-paid job. She had left her parents and
moved out at an early age to live closer to school. Since then, she never moved
back to her parents' home. It was relatively easier in her case to convince her
family that she did not want to marry or to have a boyfriend.

But the option of staying single does not always provide an easy way out.
For *lalas* who are financially independent but still living with their parents, it is
harder for them to avoid confrontations on the issue of marriage. They are less
capable of rejecting matchmaking meetings arranged by parents. It is harder
for them to move out before marriage. However, staying single is an increasingly accepted way of life in urban China among the younger and economically more capable generations. It allows a certain class of *lalas* to live outside
the institution of marriage without having to put on a heterosexual guise or
being labelled as "abnormal women".

Gaining recognition

Informants considered economic sufficiency as a prerequisite for living a life
outside a heterosexual marriage. Regardless of their age, they repeatedly
emphasized the importance of economic well-being to familial acceptance of
their same-sex relationship. Economic success brings along social respect and
recognition, according to a logic of category exchange. Being economically
successful can "save" a person from a socially undesirable category, such as
being a homosexual. Materialistic success provides one way to obtain social

and familial recognition. May believed that the high quality of life of a single woman provides a most convincing argument to her parents for her choice,

> As I'm now walking down the path of being a *lala*, I think [this argument] provides a point of convergence. First of all, I am a *lala*; secondly, I believe in celibacy. I can state firmly I won't get married because of these two factors. I'll demonstrate in various ways to my parents that I'm living well. [*As a single person?*] Yes, whether in terms of my career, my social circle and my quality of life—the reality will override all arguments. Although I can't say that I am living up to a certain standard, at least I can say that I'm not any less than anyone around my age who's married, right?[10]

Quality of life and material security are essential in constructing a successful plan for coming out. Qing listed the economic factor and the choice of partner as the two most decisive factors in a coming-out plan.

> I've thought about this problem. What would be the better situations for me? The first would be if my family members see she's good to me. The second is if my family accepts her. Because if she's to be my girlfriend, she has to be good to me, and not otherwise. Both of us should have basic material sufficiency, so that the two of us together won't have problems getting by. Otherwise it'll make it even harder for my family to accept her. After we've been together for a while, like two to three years, or even longer, then they would feel it's normal for us to be together, seeing how she takes care of me. When they feel she has become an important part of the family and that something's missing when she's not around—that would be the right time then, I think, to slowly tell my family about our situation. Right now it's still too early.[11]

Some informants believed the economic factor determines the survival of a *lala* relationship. Both Liu and Ying, one single and one married, stressed the importance of economic security. Liu said,

> I don't know what the biggest obstacle is for two women to be together. But I know, if two women have decided to be together, the best guarantee is good finances. Good finances give greater protection to the relationship . . . If you're with a woman, both of you will face many problems even with excellent finances. If you're with a man, it means everything else is in order even if you aren't financially well off—in which case the only thing you need to attend to is the relationship between the two of you.[12]

Ying said,

> I remember the first friend whom I met on the Internet told me one thing. She said, "No matter what kind of love relationship it is in this world, it still needs material support. This is especially true for this kind of relationship. There is nowhere to turn to for help. You won't be able to get help; you're all alone. If you can't even support yourself, it is extremely hard to be together." Maybe these words are too realistic, but it's true. How many love relationships are unconditional? It's impossible.[13]

The lack of other social support renders *lala* relationships vulnerable to economic conditions. Economic deprivation will further stigmatize *lalas'* already marginal existence and impose on them more difficulties in obtaining familial and social recognition. In fact, this emphasis on material success or the belief of social conformity as a prerequisite for living as a *tongzhi* echoes with the dominant discourse of social control of sexual minorities in China. Criteria of a "respectable *tongzhi*" are constructed ideologically both by state experts and within *tongzhi* communities. The economic inequality of women in China highlights the importance of material sufficiency in leading a life independent from men. The strategy of gaining social recognition by conforming to certain generally held standards of respectability indeed is developed from realistic concerns. Yet we should not overlook its possible alignment with repressive logics that work to confine *tongzhi* and other sexual minorities within heteronormative (or homonormative) boundaries. In the next chapter, I will further discuss *tongzhi* politics in China and the implications.

Heterosexual acting

Heterosexuality governs all forms of domestic and intimate relationships. Heterosexual performance is a common strategy used by informants to cover up their sexualities before their parents. Many of them have attended matchmaking meetings arranged by parents, relatives and co-workers. Although these meetings were by nature not mandatory, it would have been impolite to reject them especially if they were arranged by elders in the family or the workplace. Informants were asked to attend matchmaking meetings most frequently around the years of the so-called suitable age of marriage.

May was experienced in taking part in matchmaking meetings. Her parents and relatives were not living in Shanghai, but they still managed to arrange meetings for her through their social networks. May usually tried her best to attend and to perform well at the meetings, whether or not she had a girlfriend or not at the time. She considered attending those meetings as her obligation as a junior in the family, and a way to show her gratitude to her parents and relatives,

> I feel that even though blind dates are silly, and people are being nosy and meddlesome, if you look at this from a different angle, it is precisely because they are your relatives and your friends and care about you that they do this. If you were at this age and no one cared whether you had a boyfriend or girlfriend, if you were single or with someone, or if you ever needed a partner, then that would be scary. I think *that*, for me, would be a greater cause for fear.[14]

The pressure of marriage can last for several years. It reaches a climax when women approach their late twenties. The age of thirty is a threshold. Some informants said the pressure would begin to lessen after they turned thirty. However, since the parents of some informants were already suspicious of their daughter's sexuality, they would be even more eager to persuade their daughter to lead a "normal" heterosexual life. Chris had been under tremendous pressure since she was twenty-six. She was pressured incessantly by her mother, friends and co-workers to find a date and settle down in a marriage. The pressure mounted to a climax when she approached thirty. She finally decided to give it a trial: She began dating a man introduced to her by one of her mother's friends. Not only did she spend time with the man as a normal couple would, she also adjusted her gender expression to make it more feminine. As a self-identified *T* in the *lala* community, Chris's heterosexual acting meant a gender performance. The torturous performance lasted for almost a year. At that time, she thought the only way for her to get out of the pressure of marriage was to find a man and get married, no matter whether she loved him or not,

> It is because at that time, I thought the ultimate solution was . . . at least
> [the guy I'm dating] isn't too bad. Fine—I'll just get married! If it doesn't
> work out, then I'll get a divorce. Then at least to me, I won't have any more
> pressure. At least I was married once. And what I do after my divorce is not
> anyone's business.[15]

Marriage is a compulsory rite of passage into adulthood. There is tremendous cultural anxiety towards unmarried daughters and sons in contemporary China. Stories about how parents use different methods to persuade or force daughters to get married were abundant among my informants. During my participation in *tongzhi* activities in other cities in China, I heard different stories told by *lala* women about parents pressurizing them to get married. Some shared about how they could not divorce because of the pressure from their parents and relatives. In one sharing session at a *lala* event in Guangdong, a woman coming from a small town in northern China told us how her mother suffered from rumours spread around by neighbours and relatives about the physical well-being of her unmarried daughter. The woman was in her early thirties, and was working in another city far away from her hometown. She left her hometown because she wanted to escape the pressure of marriage. Her mother, unable to stand the rumours, had requested her daughter not to return home so often. Parents also suffer when their unmarried daughter or son face the pressure of marriage. In recent years, in Shanghai and many other cities in China, a popular form of public matchmaking participated by parents has developed. Concerned parents would post the personal information of their unmarried daughter or son in public matchmaking events, which are usually held in parks or easily accessible public spaces. Although state-imposed punishment of unmarried people is no longer as forceful and destructive as before, there remains no lack of worried parents.

Coping with Marriage

Married *lalas* have been increasingly visible as a distinctive and significant group in local *lala* communities in China. Online message boards dedicated to married *lalas* are increasing in number. Many discussions and articles about this group are being put up on the Internet, and greater attention has been directed to the specific needs of this group.

Likewise, married *lala* women are growing in number in the local communities of Shanghai. A few whom I met in *lala* gatherings were in their thirties, and some had kids. For married *lala* informants, the pressure mainly came from three sources: namely, the natal family, the conjugal family, and their extramarital same-sex relationship. The married *lalas* whom I came into contact with belonged to two groups: those who had started having a same-sex relationship before marriage, and those who started or only realized their desire after getting married. Chris (thirty years old), Ling (twenty-seven years old) and Tan (twenty-seven years old) had started their same-sex relationships before their marriage. At the time of interview, they were either planning or were already in cooperative marriage. Ying (in her early thirties) had also had same-sex relationships before and after her marriage. Mu (thirty-three years old), Coral (in her early thirties) and Heng (thirty-six years old) belonged to the second group. They started having same-sex relationships after marriage. Their coping strategies, either to maintain their current marriage or to survive the pressure to get married, can be categorized into three major ways: 1. secret dual life: hiding their same-sex extramarital relationship from their husband and natal family; 2. making it open: initiating open or semi-open negotiation with husbands; 3. faking it: having a cooperative marriage with a gay man. Informants sometimes adopted more than one strategy at one time or applied different strategies at different stages. For example, one might lead a secret dual life at the beginning of her extramarital relationship, and only attempt to reach some kind of mutual agreement with her husband at a later time. Or one might juggle between her natal family and her secret same-sex relationship for a long time, and only strive to live independently from her parents' control after a cooperative marriage. At the time of the interview, Ying and Coral were struggling in a stressful dual life. Mu and Heng were having open and semi-open negotiations with their husbands to accommodate their extramarital same-sex relationships. Chris, Ling and Tan, the three younger informants, had chosen the least confrontational but most experimental method: arranging a cooperative marriage.

Secret dual life

Ying and Coral, both in their early thirties, had chosen to leave their hometowns and husbands for a temporary stay in Shanghai. Physical distance seemed to be very important for them in striking a balance between their marriage and extramarital same-sex relationship.

Both of them talked about the difficulties of maintaining a same-sex relationship outside of marriage. Coral lived with her girlfriend during her temporary stay in Shanghai. She expressed how every day she felt tortured by the triangular relationship and how difficult it was to have a divorce,

> Within a year, my husband knew [of my extramarital relationship] . . . Now I believe that a married woman should not . . . love another woman. If I had known three years ago that it would end up like this, no matter how much I loved her, I would have controlled [my feelings] because you end up hurting three persons. All three persons end up in pain. If I had known it would turn out like this, I would rather have endured a bit of heartache in the beginning. It really is devastating . . . She's in a lot of pain now. She feels she has no security. I can't give her much security and I can't make any promises. On the other hand, my husband is also suffering because I cannot give him what a normal man would have. I've suffered a lot as well. Sometimes I just want to live simply, to not feel any burden when I open my eyes in the morning, to have the simple joys of smiling, working, reading. Now every morning when I open my eyes, I feel a heavy load, a dead weight . . . At that time, I wanted a divorce. I talked with my husband about getting a divorce. He was very forbearing. He said, "Don't worry. Just do what you need to do. It doesn't matter. There's no need to worry about me. I'll always be here if you decide to come back." If he hadn't been so accommodating, I would have been more determined to get a divorce, but his attitude has rendered me helpless to do anything about it.[16]

Similarly, Ying's husband did not want to get a divorce even though their relationship had never been easy since the first day of marriage. They still pretended to be a normal couple in front of family and friends. It seems that the social cost of getting a divorce can be even higher than suffering in a bad marriage. This probably explains the consistently low divorce rates in China over the years.[17]

Making it open

Mu was in her mid-thirties and had a child. She had a girlfriend living overseas. Mu's girlfriend was also married. Both of their husbands knew of their relationship, and both husbands tolerated it for similar reasons. Mu said the geographical distance and her lover's gender made it easier for her husband to accept it,

What was his reaction? He was taken by surprise. It was like, he could write a story about his life. How could something like this happen to him? But since it's happened, and the other party is a woman, her being of the same sex poses less of a threat to him. And with the distance between us, he came to accept it. He wouldn't have if it had been a man. It was the same with her husband. He thinks two women can't really do anything! (Laughs.) But her husband was really angry at first . . . really angry. How could his wife be involved in an affair? And later when he found out it's with a woman, he came to accept it gradually. "[18]

When asked whether she had considered getting a divorce, Mu named having children and economic viability as the two most important deciding factors:

Children are an important deciding factor. If you don't have children, you can get a divorce without having much to trouble about, as long as both parties figure out the finances. But if children are involved, [a divorce] would affect them a great deal. We absolutely do not have the right to pursue our own pleasure at the expense of a child's future or happiness. Economic reasons are part of the consideration; but the child will also be affected personally. And this will have adverse effects on the child's growth and well-being. We cannot impinge upon a child's future just to fulfil our own happiness. This is one very important deciding factor. Of course there's also the economic factor—let's say, if it's not economically viable for two people to be together, then there'll be a lot of tension. And tension results in fighting and breakup. If after putting in tremendous energy and effort into being together, two people are still going to be separated, then the stakes are too high. There's no point to [staying together].[19]

Heng, also a mother, experienced considerable freedom in her marriage. She and her husband were only maintaining their marriage for the sake of their young child. Both of them were having extramarital relationships at the time of interview. Heng stayed in the marriage because she did not want her deteriorating relationship with her husband to affect her child. Her husband had also rejected her request for custody of their child in the event of a divorce.

With varying degrees of mutual consent from their husbands, both Heng and Mu managed to accommodate their same-sex relationships within their heterosexual marriages.

Faking it: Cooperative marriage

The cooperative marriage is an increasingly popular coping strategy among younger informants in my research. At least three relatively younger informants who were married or about-to-get married saw cooperative marriage as the way to cope with the pressure of marriage.

Cooperative marriage is not new to *lalas* and gay men in urban China. Back when I first started my research in Shanghai, I had already heard of the idea of cooperative marriages, and had heard rumours of couples seeking this form of union. But when I returned to the city in 2006 and 2007, I heard real-life stories of people being in cooperative marriages. Later, I found that some women whom I had met or interviewed earlier were planning to have or were already in cooperative marriages themselves. In less than two years, the once experimental idea had been enthusiastically put to test in real life. Its rising popularity in such a short period of time reflects *lalas* and gay men's desperation to put an end to the everyday struggle of covering up their desires and same-sex relationships. Its popularity can also be attributed to the ever-expanding *tongzhi* cyber community in China. Both Ling and Chris found their "husbands" on the Internet. Ling searched advertisements posted by gay men looking for a marriage partner and Chris posted an advertisement themselves on lesbian or gay websites. The process resembles conventional matchmaking, except in this case, it is for a performed marriage between a *lala* and a gay man. Typically, one party posts an online advertisement and waits for a response. A meeting is then arranged between both parties, and is usually attended by same-sex partners on both sides. Ling, Chris and Tan all brought up how a cooperative marriage is not only a matter affecting the *lala* and gay man involved, but is essentially a union that will affect their respective partners. In effect, it becomes a marriage of (at least) four people. If all parties consider it a good match after the first meeting, they will start to detail their plan to meet families of the male and female sides as regular couples do. If both families accept them as their daughter or son's possible mate, then they will proceed to marital arrangements: living arrangements, regular visits to parents of both parties, financial arrangements and so on.

Ling was a Shanghai native and lived with her parents. In preparation for her cooperative marriage, she had spent over a year "dating" her future husband. During this time, her gay marriage partner spent much time with her family as her boyfriend. Her family accepted the gay partner. At the time of the interview, Ling and he had just registered for marriage. They were planning a wedding banquet, and had showed off their "newly bought" apartment to their families, which was actually the home of the gay partner and his same-sex partner. Ling was to stay with her own same-sex partner in a rented apartment after marriage. She said marriage was the only way for her to move out from her parents' home and to live away from their day-to-day scrutiny. She believed that her parents would not need to cope with her sexuality after she got married. For Ling, it was impossible for them to accept or understand homosexuality.

Ling and Tan were a couple. Tan was also thinking about getting married at the time of interview. She had already come out to her mother. Her mother had once implied to Ling that she would rather Tan have a fake marriage than stay unmarried and in a same-sex relationship. Ling recalled this conversation with Tan's mother,

> Actually, her mother has talked to me about this issue before. She hopes that I would talk to [Tan]. Even though they know the marriage is fake, they don't want the groom's side of the family to know—that is, it's better to sort of have a half-son who can get along with the family and live happily together, and to feign ignorance about the whole situation and her role in it. Her mother feels that if everyone knew it was a fake deal, it would be really embarrassing, so it's better to pretend not to know.[20]

Therefore, Tan was thinking about finding a marriage partner and following what Ling had done. She saw it as a way to save her parents from social pressure,

> They care most about what people say about them. They're concerned about their relationship with their relatives. They feel that if [my marriage] can be managed appropriately, then problem solved. They think, once the problem's solved, the two of you can move out; people won't be so concerned about you anymore, and as parents, we can relax.[21]

Chris, one of the first *lala* women I met in Shanghai in 2005, told me in 2007 she was thinking of having a cooperative marriage. She was almost thirty when I first met her, and was under severe pressure from her family to get married. She had found a suitable gay partner on the Internet, and her wedding banquet was coming up at the time of interview. Chris's girlfriend was fully involved in the planning of her cooperative marriage, and they were planning to live together after the wedding. The news was a relief to her parents, since for a number of years, they had been suspicious of their daughter's sexual orientation. Yet for Chris, even with full control of the occasion, it was a marriage that she would rather never happen.

Strategizing Marriage

Informants dealt with their parents in two common ways: using more recognized social identities to compensate for their unaccepted sexuality, and employing a heterosexual disguise.

Married *lalas* suffer the most as they are doubly burdened by their natal and conjugal families. Many *lalas* are forced to live a dual life and to hide their extramarital same-sex relationships and desires under the guise of a heterosexual marriage. The newly emergent form of lesbian and gay union—in a cooperative marriage between a *lala* and a gay man—is an experimental

way for non-normative sexual subjects to survive the everyday intimate surveillance of their families. In the present social and cultural context of China,
cooperative marriage is understood by participants as a performative union
which conforms to parents' expectations. It is also an act of "in-ing" (into the
heteronormative model) that gives space for the existence of their same-sex
relationships.

Lala informants in this study demonstrate how sexually non-normative
women in China actively struggle for spaces between the heterosexual
marriage and same-sex relationship. Some employ a spatial strategy of leaving
their conjugal homes and the familial obligations attached and starting their
same-sex relationship in a new city, even if only for a brief interim. More and
more *lala* women of the one-child generation (born after the 1980s) are engaging
in the self-directed heterosexual performance of cooperative marriages. The
new spaces and forms of *lala* household and family they have created constitute
an emerging *tongzhi* private sphere that can offer alternative models and discourses to the heteronormative model of intimacy. The day-to-day operations
of this new form of *tongzhi* family unit, its legal implications and its effectiveness as a form of spatial politics for *lalas* and gay men are yet to be examined.
The following chapter features further discussion on cooperative marriages.

Chapter 5
A Smile on the Surface: The Politics of Public Correctness

A fake marriage is a promise between ourselves and our families. On the surface we keep a smile, but the sacrifices we make are more than anyone can imagine. (Dudu, "Why don't we come out?" les+, Volume 09, May 2007, p. 33; original text in Chinese)[1]

In this chapter, I look at the social, political and cultural contexts that have led to the emergence of a *tongzhi* politics, which I term "the politics of public correctness". I also look at the various ways in which *lalas* put this politics into real-life practice, including through the increasingly popular practice of "cooperative marriage". Through this discussion, I intend to bring into view culturally specific forms of homophobia that are practised in the domains of family and public discourse of homosexuality in contemporary China. The discourse of "Chinese tolerance" of homosexuality, in particular, usually defined in opposition to the physical expressions of homophobia in the West, continues to circulate widely as a nationalistic narrative countering the Western imagination of a homophobic (and thus "backward") China. I will demonstrate how tolerance, as a silent force, serves as an effective discourse of sexual regulation in contemporary Chinese families. I will argue that it is problematic for non-normative sexual subjects and scholars to engage continually in this essentialist and illusory notion of "Chinese tolerance". This silent repression, especially felt by *lalas* and gay men in their heterosexual families, has generated culturally specific forms of resistance and the construction of the very meaning of "resistance".

Closely related to "tolerance", "normalization" is another dominant discourse that is circulating in China, and is particularly promoted by state experts who work to advocate a "proper" and "scientific" understanding of homosexuality and homosexuals (as discussed in Chapter 2). The project to normalize homosexuals can be understood as a response to the decades-long institutional stigmatization of homosexuals in China. It can also be interpreted as part of a greater project to construct a new sexual morality for the newly capitalized and increasingly commodified society. The main goal is to draw up a definition of what is understood as "properly gay", as discussed by Lisa Rofel (2007).[2] Or in other words, the normalization project is a critical site for examining the interaction between notions of hetero- (Warner 1991) and homo-normativities (Duggan 2003), how heterosexual norms are interpreted as the universal standard, and how a new order of homonormativity is taking shape in contemporary China.

Social Context

The politics of public correctness is best exemplified by the recurring themes in *tongzhi* community discourse of calling for a "healthy" (*jiankang*) and "sunny" (*yangguang*) lifestyle and positive representation. The general belief is that one has to "stand up" (*zhanqilai*), to be a socially respectable person, before she can go public as a *tongzhi*. In other words, it is believed that being "correct" in public—being a law-abiding citizen, an economically productive member of society, an obedient daughter and a "model" homosexual (that is, one who fits into the homonormative imagination of "healthy" and "sunny" representations)—will bring about positive recognition by one's family, and eventually, acceptance by the general public. In recent years, the public sphere has been influenced by a forceful and evolving discourse of *tongzhi* visibility and rights. At the same time, the family institution in China has gradually replaced state authorities as the chief monitor of people's private lives in the post-reform period. I will look into the sociopolitical context that has enabled the family, both as an institution and a physical entity, to turn into an effective agent of social control over non-heterosexual subjects. With a critical understanding of the historical context that has empowered the family to be an effective hetero-sexual gatekeeper, we stand in a better position to discuss the implications of the politics of public correctness to *lalas* in contemporary China.

The repressive nature of the family has been mentioned by many research-ers in their studies of the homosexual population in China (Li 2002; Li and Wang 1992; Rofel 1999; Chou 1997; Chou 2000). That said, we cannot take it as self-evident that the Chinese family is always repressive to sexually deviant members, or that it has been repressive in identical ways at all times. Nor has the notion of what constitutes a "Chinese family" always been the same and stable over time. The current socioeconomic and political development of China has played a major role in maintaining and transforming the repressive and the productive sides of the heterosexual family institution towards homo-sexual subjects. The politics of public correctness can be better understood as a response to the changing contours of social control of sexual deviants in the public and private domains in post-reform China. One of the major transforma-tions, as we have seen throughout this book, is within the paradigm of control over one's private life, which has shifted from a direct and all-imposing state control—through *danwei* and neighbourhood surveillance—to an intimate day-to-day scrutiny executed by one's family through the language of love and care. The control of sexual deviants in the family sphere is exercised through a compulsory system of reciprocal care and love between parents and children. The provision of mutual love and care is always justified and legitimated by a reference to the Confucian value of filial piety, which is generally held uncontested as a traditional Chinese value. It is also used to justify the collective participation of parents and relatives in one's marriage, which is considered not solely as a personal matter, but a duty one owes to both family and society. The discourse of filial piety—together with the cultural belief in "keeping face" (*aimianzi*), which extended to a family, refers to the maintenance of harmony at the surface—puts sexually non-normative subjects in a disadvantaged discursive position. Resisting subjects will find it hard to draw upon cultural resources to free them from the compulsory participation to maintain surface harmony in their families.[3]

In Chou Wah Shan and Li Yinhe's studies of the homosexual population in China, they analysed ways of repression against homosexual subjects in the Chinese society and family (Chou 1997; Chou 2000; Li 2002; Li and Wang 1992). To Chou, the silent repression by the Chinese family and society is coped with using a set of culturally specific strategies. Chou summarizes them as non-confrontational, not sex-centred, non-hetero-/homo-based and traditional Chinese value-oriented (Chou 2000). Li also believes that the dominant mode of repression against homosexual subjects in China is not "ruthless persecution and extreme hostility" such as that in the West, but "ignorance and prejudice in the mainstream society" (Li 2002, p. 406). Li explains how this, for many homosexual subjects in China, has led to a coping strategy of being non-confrontational and escapist. The belief of a more "tolerant" Chinese culture towards homosexuality, usually with reference to the more physical forms of homophobic expression in the West, is a popular contemporary reinterpretation of traditional Chinese culture upheld by many both within the academia and *tongzhi* communities in China. Many informants of this study also shared this belief. The following comment on Chinese perceptions of homosexuality made by May, who was in her mid-twenties, is representative of the attitude held by many informants:

> It's probably good that China and its culture are not extreme. After all, it is a patriarchal society and no one is particularly sensitive to the oppression experienced by lesbians or gay men. Everyone seems to lead a stable life. Many gay men and lesbians proceed to get married when it's time to do so. One's pain and suffering, one's desolation—all is stashed away in a hidden corner, never to be exposed under the bright sunlight. Everyone

thinks if you can't see it then it doesn't exist. That's why no one cares about these issues much; these issues only come up gradually and occasionally, only if some *tongzhi* bar got too racy and got shut down, or if two persons went an extra mile to get married—just like that, just another piece of news coverage. People don't really care much about the things that really happen among us [*lalas*]. Basically, I think standards are still quite relaxed. If you can manage your own feelings and find your own path, you won't run into much of a problem. At least you won't have the feeling of fearing for your life which you sometimes get living in a foreign country.[4]

The silent, non-physical repression of non-normative sexuality enacted within the family is sometimes interpreted as a kind of cultural tolerance towards homosexuality in China. But this form of repression not only silences the repressed subjects, but also erases them entirely from sight. Silence can be a violent form of symbolic erasure. As understood by May and many other informants, their existence in society is always a shadowy one at the "hidden corner". This is a form of symbolic violence that can be misread as cultural tolerance. We can only say that the form of repression is culturally different in the Chinese context and it might generate an entirely different framework of survival strategies and understanding of what constitutes a political *tongzhi* subjectivity.

Taiwan scholars Liu Jen-peng and Ding Naifei have responded critically to Chou's celebration of Chinese tolerance towards homosexuality. In their work, they reveal the inherent violence done against homosexual subjects through this silent tolerance (Liu and Ding 2005). They argue that the "poetic of reticence", as essentialized by Chou as the Chinese way of tolerance, is itself a kind of violence that deprives homosexual subjects of any speaking and visible position:

> The order of things whereby some things are more speakable than others and therefore allow those unspeakable things to remain in the shadow "where they belong"—*this* order is what is preserved.
>
> We further suggest that cooperating in the preservation of such an order has itself homophobic effects to the extent that its very preservation in a narrative as influential as Chou's will allow for the continued spawning of just this sort of benevolence and reticent good will, with its especial containing force in the areas of personal sexual and affective behaviour. Chou writes as if containment itself (*baorong*) were not in this particular "Chinese" space/time a sufficiently effective form of homophobia and discrimination. (p. 49)

In reality, in addition to the symbolic violence theorized by Liu and Ding, violence against homosexuals in China—whether in the form of hate speech, domestic violence (including spousal and parental abuse) or institutional repression—is prevalent in everyday life, as reported by the media and personally witnessed by the informants in this research. What further makes tolerance an insufficient response towards non-normative sexual subjects is the rapid development of an identity-based *tongzhi* community and its increasingly articulate efforts in obtaining an exclusive same-sex lifestyle that is *not secondary* to a visible normative heterosexual relationship, as is the case within the framework of silent tolerance. The emergence of sexually identified communities has transformed the relationship between the heterosexual family institution and homosexual individuals in significant ways. Since the late 1990s when community networking first appeared on the Internet, the self-understanding and expectations of homosexual subjects have transformed dramatically. The period saw the emergence of a self-empowering and rights-conscious community discourse which had been absent during the early half of the decade when Chou and Li carried out their research. Those developments have intensified the conflict between *lala* subjects and the heterosexual family institution.

In the context of an omnipresent discursive struggle against the dominant Western (mis)interpretation of non-West societies and cultures as well as the hegemony of the Western framework of lesbian and gay activism, the belief of a more tolerant Chinese culture towards homosexuality can be understood as a form of cultural resistance and a redefinition exercised by the local society. An enormous amount of effort has been put into constructing a history of homosexuality and a *tongzhi* politics that are different from those of the West. However, I argue that cultural resistance cannot be used to justify any belief which refuses to acknowledge non-physical forms of repression, and more importantly, conveniently ignores the fact that physical violence against sexually non-normative people does occur in contemporary China. In other words, if we agree that "tolerance", when defined as a "silent sanction" or the Chinese version of "don't tell, don't ask"—to borrow anthropologist Elisabeth Lund Engebretsen's (2009) comparison—is also a kind of homophobia, then we need to further acknowledge the fact that "tolerance" in contemporary China cannot be understood at all times as a "silent" or "mild" position, and that in fact it is aligned with other more physically expressed and visible forms of homophobic acts. Furthermore, tolerance is a discourse of depoliticization and personalization of political issues, as suggested by Wendy Brown (2006). In the domain of sexuality (and also gender) in contemporary China, it has successfully displaced radical questioning of the logic that distinguishes the tolerable and the intolerable, and the positions of the tolerator and the tolerated, with the discourse of personal failure (one's failure to conform to collective norms). Or worse, Chinese tolerance works to invoke feelings of shame in the sexually non-normative subjects through the family's "silent tolerance". As experienced by informants in their coming out to their parents, the topics of homosexuality and one's non-normative sexual desire are forbidden tin the household.

Tolerance is only granted if one abides by the law of silence and internalizes the association of shame and her sexuality. If ever there is tolerance towards homosexuality in Chinese culture, it is a tolerance that comes with conditions. Brown (ibid.) suggests that the politics of tolerance "involves two kinds of boundary drawing and a practice of licensing". The two forms of boundary drawing are the "spatial boundaries of dominion and relevance, as well as moral boundaries about what can and cannot be accommodated within this domain" (p. 29). The "licensing practices" imposed on non-normative sexual subjects in Chinese families include self-shaming and keeping themselves silent and invisible. Tolerance is only to be granted when the surface order and harmony of the heterosexual family is not disrupted. Silence, as Liu and Ding argue, is the only language permitted in order to keep everyone in place within the heterosexual order. I would add that self-shaming is the only emotion non-normative sexual subjects are permitted to express concerning their sexuality in the family space. Self-shaming is most often imposed on non-normative sexual subjects as a result of their "failure" to keep their family's face and to pursue heterosexual marriage and reproduction, even though many informants expressed personal aspirations of having a same-sex marriage, or setting up a family with their female partners. Informants often used the concept of saving the family's or their parent's face to describe the surface order of their family. It is the very meaning of "to keep a smile at the surface". A non-confrontational strategy of coming out, coming out "softly" (*ruan chugui*, as discussed in Chapter 3), not coming out to parents at all, and the cooperative marriage are ways *lalas* use to maintain this surface order. When justifying their choices, informants usually employed the same language of love and care which has ironically kept them out of sight from the family space. Thus informants appropriated individual sacrifice and suffering, hiding their same-sex desires and relationships from their parents and engaging in cooperative or involuntary marriages in the name of filial piety. They were thus responding to the repressive force of the heterosexual family using the same cultural logic by which they were repressed.

Outside the family, the politics of public correctness is also a response to a long history of state-imposed medical, moral and legal stigmatization of homosexual subjects. The decades-long pathological treatment of people engaged in homosexual activities and punishments executed by the legal and the social security authorities before and after the abolishment of the crime of hooliganism in 1997 have impressed upon society that homosexuality is associated with mental and moral degradation. To many in the newly emerged *tongzhi* communities, destigmatization assumes priority before other goals. Alongside the effort to enhance *tongzhi* visibility, local *tongzhi* groups are struggling to reclaim a more socially acceptable image of homosexuals. The abolishment of hooliganism in the new Criminal Law in 1997 and the depathologization of homosexuality as a mental disorder in 2001 have paved the way for the active participation of state experts, particularly from the academia, medical and legal domains, in the construction of new authoritative discourses of homosexuality. Experts' participation in the new discursive construction of homosexuality is also part of a bigger project calling for a scientific study of sexuality. A scientific attitude towards sex has been promoted in the country since the economic reform era. During the 1990s, the threat of HIV/AIDS to public health again called for the participation of medical experts in a national campaign of new sexual morality. Under this social context, state experts, especially medical professionals, stepped up as the most eligible candidates to lead a new scientific study on sexual deviance. A group of sympathetic medical professionals launched the first journal in the country on homosexuality in 1998. Entitled the *Friend Exchange* (*Pengyou tongxin*), it was circulated within *tongzhi* communities and among concerned medical experts. In the inaugural issue, contributing experts write about how they regard it as their undeniable responsibility to society to engage in an anti-discrimination campaign:

> Homosexuals often hope to live with someone who loves them as much as they love them. Due to the backward development of our society, a lot of homosexuals have to resort to a promiscuous lifestyle under pressure from the discrimination they face. It makes it very difficult for them to have stable, reliable and good monogamous relationships, and difficult for them to find a suitable partner. For many of them, they have no alternative but to have sexual relations with strangers in order to fulfil their biological drive and deeper psychological needs. This situation makes them highly susceptible to HIV infection and sexually transmitted diseases. Hence, in this era of AIDS, it is the grave responsibility of the scholarly community to change the social conditions and discriminating environment for homosexuals. (*Friend Exchange*, 1998, pp. 4–5; quoted from Chou 2000, p. 302; original text in Chinese)[5]

An increasing number of experts have actively taken part in the project to normalize homosexuality since the late 1990s. From the above quotation, we can see that "homosexuals" refer only to male homosexuals based on the sexual practices it describes which are generally stereotyped to be belonged to the male homosexuals. They are perceived as the victims of society's "backward development" as they are forced to engage in promiscuous sex for the sake of keeping anonymous and are exposed to the threat of sexually transmitted diseases and HIV infection. Gay sexuality is conceptualized as a threat to public health and morality. Gay lifestyle, especially the practice of having sex with strangers or with multiple sexual partners, is put in opposition to "stable, reliable and good monogamous relationships". This represents a dominant attitude shared by many other "sympathetic" state experts. They acknowledge the widespread social prejudice against homosexuals and the negative effect prejudice has on the individual homosexual. However, dominant heterosexual norms are still conceived as the universal standard, and therefore as outlining the most desirable form of human sexual relations. The discourse of normalization therefore fails to discern its own homophobic logic. Similarly, it calls for a "tolerance" that only reinforces the dominant hegemonic norms and categories of inclusion/exclusion. By demanding homosexuals to conform to dominant sexual norms, the discourse of normalization might succeed in removing long-held negative stereotypes of homosexuals in society, yet it also leads to a depoliticizing effect that disables the questioning of those very norms, social forces and institutions that continue to sustain systems of social exclusion.

Medical, academic and legal experts have served as official advisors and organizers for *tongzhi* hotlines and working groups in different cities. The active participation of state experts in the destigmatization campaign can also be explained by the specific political context of China. Cooperating with state experts or their affiliated state institutions can ensure political and financial security of the project or working group concerned. The presence of experts can also be advantageous in conducting effective communication with the general public. Experts are aware of their strategic role in the campaign of anti-discrimination. Another issue of *Friend Exchange* elaborates the expert's role in a model of cooperation with the state,

> On the other hand, there is a need to popularize the liberation regarding sexual orientation. Denmark, the Scandinavian country, has achieved this by first having homosexual organizations connecting with the academia; from there, academics began to communicate with the government, and the government in turn advised the public on homosexual issues. China is following in the footsteps of Scandinavia because the situation there is closer to that of China: That is, to build a cooperative relationship with the government, to galvanize everyone including those with variant perspectives and attitudes to better tackle China's issues on homosexuality. [China also needs to] take into perspective scientific knowledge, and foster public understanding and acceptance of homosexuals, eradicate discrimination, and furthermore, to create a productive dialogue with homosexuals in general. (*Friend Exchange*, December Issue, 2002, p. 44; original text in Chinese)[6]

In this respect, state experts have played a major role in creating a new discursive space for a normalized homosexual subject position, as opposed to the medical-driven and moralistic understandings in the past.

"Walking under the Sunlight with Pride!"

At the community level, the politics of public correctness is demonstrated in the popular use of "healthy" and "sunny" to envision an ideal form of *tongzhi* existence and public representation. In the first issue of *les+*, a community magazine started in 2005 by a group of young *lalas* in Beijing, the slogan on the cover communicates their aspiration of life,

> After the darkness fades away, I'll be holding your hand, walking under the sunlight with pride, boldly and happily living our lives! (*les+*, Issue one, 2005; original text in Chinese)[7]

"Darkness" and "sunlight" in this slogan symbolize two contrasting periods of time: the stigmatized past and the hopeful present. The new generation of urban *lalas* is looking forward to a non-shadowy future and a proud *tongzhi* subjectivity. The divide of darkness and light is sometimes applied to the spatial difference between the cyberspace and offline worlds. Community members are used to referring to the offline world as reality (*xianshi*). There has been a constant effort in the community to extend cyber activities into the "real" world—thereby expanding community social life from darkness to broad daylight. The symbolic use of darkness/brightness and the emphasis on a proud *tongzhi* subjectivity tie in with the struggle for visibility and positive representation in the context of social stigmatization.

State experts wield a significant role in building up a positive *tongzhi* image both within and outside the community in this normalization project. They represent an authoritative voice calling for a positive *tongzhi* subjecthood which highlights "self-respect" (*zizun*) and "self-discipline" (*zilü*). The following extract, also cited from the December issue (2002) of *Friend Exchange*, represents the dominant attitude of sympathetic state experts towards homosexual subjects:

> Among homosexuals in China, there are many who are highly cultured, who aspire to better lives and who work tirelessly to fulfil their life's worth. Some homosexuals who are now leading "pretty decent lives" once worked very hard to climb the ladder in society. It was after they had achieved a level of success and made contributions to their parents and families that they found the courage to discuss their sexual orientation. Some homosexuals believe that the underlying meaning of being a homosexual is to first be a person—a person with basic human dignity. Possessing dignity has nothing to do with homosexuality.
>
> Furthermore, there are homosexuals who say that as a homosexual, one should advocate for self-discipline. Only with the buttress of self-discipline and responsibility do we have the right to ask for tolerance and kind treatment from the public and the government. If there is no attempt at self-discipline, there is nowhere to begin. One must always demonstrate self-discipline if one is to win recognition from the public—this has always been the case for nations, communities, down to the individual citizen. As a community who is still struggling to gain public recognition, homosexuals must all the more attend to their personal image, striving towards establishing a healthy and respectable image in society. We can strive

towards this goal even as perfection cannot be obtained in every aspect. We need to assume societal roles, to obey the law, to cultivate integrity, to discipline ourselves and to take up personal responsibilities. Only when we are responsible for ourselves can we be responsible for others, and for the society, and through that, win recognition from the public. (*Friend Exchange*, December Issue, 2002, p. 49; original text in Chinese)[8]

"Self-discipline" and "a healthy and respectable image in society" are considered the prerequisites to public acceptance of homosexuality. Here, the logic of public correctness, expressed through the language of social conformity and responsibility, is used to justify social recognition of homosexual subjects. In other words, one has to first become a model citizen before she can ask for "tolerance" and "fair treatment" from society and the authorities. This kind of moralistic discourse of "good homosexuals" can be better understood against the backdrop of what Rofel terms as the construction of "post-socialist subjects" in post-Mao China (Rofel 2007). The formation of "post-socialist subjects" demands "the positive development of desire", or in other words, "the proper balance between interest and passion" (ibid., p. 14) so as not to threaten the success of the economic reform. Put another way, the regulation of desire and the construction of "proper" sexual subjectivity are what constitute the notion of "cultural citizenship" in post-socialist China. Rofel argues that "class identity" and "culture" have replaced political struggles as the major sites where citizenship is defined and negotiated. The construction of cultural citizenship has inaugurated the negotiation of new sexual norms and hierarchical differences (ibid., p. 94). The hierarchies of difference, or the system of inclusion/exclusion of homosexuals as expressed by the experts, are clearly discernible: "Good homosexuals" are those who come to terms with the dominant sex ideals, which stress stability and a monogamous relationship. "Good homosexuals" are not threatening to public health, social security and morality, and hence should be "tolerated" and even recognized as part of the new cultural citizenship project.

The same reasoning of public correctness is echoed in *tongzhi* communities. An operator of a *lala* hotline in Shanghai explained to me why the hotline has an underlying stance of "not showing encouragement to homosexuality" (*buguli lichang*), especially to callers who are at school age.

> We won't say that there's nothing wrong, that [the caller] is absolutely right, or that she can do whatever she wants. We usually tackle problem by problem. If she introduces herself as a student, we'll tell her she should focus more on her studies as that has nothing to do with her sexual orientation. It has everything to do with her life. If you cannot do well on things that matter to you the most, how can you bring happiness to another person? (Interviewer: *That is to say, to finish school first?*) You can date when you're still in school but you cannot give up everything for this. If you

cannot even focus on yourself and take steps to improve your life, then you won't be able to give another person happiness and security.[9]

In the above case, homosexuality is not encouraged if one is not recognized as a self-sustaining social member. Such attitudes also underlie the widespread intolerance of school-aged *lalas* in the *tongzhi* community. They are regarded as ineligible sexual beings. This echoes the widespread social disavowal of "premature" dating and sexuality (*zaolian*, or literally, "early love") in contemporary China. Homosexual youths are further disadvantaged as they are dismissed by both their age and non-normative sexuality. Here, the influence of the deep-rooted social stigmatization against homosexual subjects and the internal regulation of visibility/invisibility in the *tongzhi* community become clearly manifest.

The politics of public correctness is well demonstrated in the community's understanding of coming out and in members' justification of cooperative marriages. As discussed in Chapter 3, coming out is generally considered as an *option* rather than a politically correct *obligation* in China. Some even refute coming out as a responsible act as it can bring tremendous harm to one's family. To many informants, being a considerate and filial daughter is far more important than being honest to their parents. Coming out is regarded as a process that requires strategic planning, and one which can last for a prolonged period of time. A non-confrontational and well-planned coming out is always preferred over any impulsive and direct ones. And if one has to come out to her family, the quality of her same-sex relationship and of her partner (that is, whether she is good-natured, economically self-sufficient and recognized as professionally accomplished) will all be taken as prerequisites for the very act. There is an underlying two-step model to coming out: first, to stand up as a "model" member of society, and then, to come out as a "less desirable" sexual being. It echoes with the experts' call to perform one's socially assigned roles well before demanding recognition from family and society. The ultimate goal again is to preserve the surface order of the family and society as a whole.

Cooperative Marriage

Cooperative marriage is the most elaborate form of the politics of public correctness. In theory, a cooperative marriage can be practised by people with all kinds of sexualities and intentions. What I discuss here is the cooperative marriage performed specifically by a *lala* and a gay man, in which both parties are fully aware of the ritualized nature of their relationship.

In view of the much stronger force of social conformity in the pre-reform period, members in *tongzhi* communities generally hold that similar forms of consensual performance of marital relationship have existed long before the present notion of cooperative marriage. But the easy accessibility of social contacts and the abundant supply of potential marriage partners have only been recently made possible by the presence of self-identified sexual communities. I suggest that the development of lesbian and gay communities in China has largely facilitated the practice of cooperative marriage. The existence of these communities has not only allowed individuals to identify potential marriage partners, but also provided the essential information, group support and protection for participants in a cooperative marriage.

Attitudes towards cooperative marriage in the *tongzhi* community in China are divided. Many are sceptical of whether it can be put into practice in real life. For the limited number of pioneers who are already practising it, the outcomes of this experimental form of union are yet to be known. This book's discussion of cooperative marriage is an early attempt to understand an experiment that has just begun to take shape; the fact that cooperative marriage is taking place at a time when the lives of *lalas* and gay people in urban China are so changeable and conducive to external influence means that observations made in this book are necessarily fleeting and fragmented. That being said, I aim to offer readers a glimpse into such pioneer attempts. I also offer my preliminary analysis of the possible impacts of cooperative marriage on lesbian and gay individuals and the *tongzhi* community as a whole.

In the case of cooperative marriage, we see that the silent force of repression within the contemporary Chinese family institution is met with the same silent force of resistance. Cooperative marriages do not challenge the institutions that subject homosexual subjects to invisibility in the first place. Rather, as John Cho argues in his study of contract marriage in South Korea, it has the effect of "erasing the subjectivities and agency of Korean gays and lesbians as social subjects" (Cho, 2009).[10] Many in the *tongzhi* community in China also echo this concern. They regard cooperative marriages as a compromise rather than a politically sound strategy which brings forthright recognition to homosexual subjects. Some are sceptical of its effectiveness: given the closeness that is expected between in-laws and the married couple in China, some do not believe that the cooperative marriage is a realistic option. Others worry about the demand of grandchildren from parents on both sides. The pressure of childbearing is particularly felt by *lalas* and gay men who are the only child in the family. It is much more difficult for them to reject their parents' request to carry on the family line. Also, the legal complexities are hard to resolve in the case of a long-term cooperative marriage. These include the conjugal financial arrangement, the legal obligation of both parties to take care of each other and even their in-laws as stated in the Marriage Law, and spousal rights that prioritize marital partners over other forms of kinship in cases of emergency. Zhou Dan, a gay legal activist and practising lawyer based in Shanghai, told me in an interview in 2010 that in recent years, he has received a constant flow of lesbian and gay individuals seeking legal consultation on cooperative marriages. While the number of people seeking advice is still very small (less than ten people every year), the number has increased steadily from year to year. Many marriage partners will draft a legal statement on financial arrangements before their wedding. But according to Zhou, the complexities of a cooperative marriage are not restricted to finances; and not everything can be settled by legal means. For example, interpersonal relationship issues that may arise with the in-laws are unlikely to be settled legally. The biggest uncertainty or risk in the cooperative marriage is that one can never exhaust all possible complications before the marriage. Apart from legal concerns, many are unable to overcome the ethical dilemma brought about by cooperative marriage. To many, the fact that one has to deceive one's parents (and relatives, co-workers, other associates) for a supposedly prolonged period of time is a major drawback of cooperative marriage.

Cooperative marriages fully appropriate the surface order of the heterosexual family through an extreme performance of normative heterosexuality. It is a coping strategy responding directly to the heterosexual policing by the family through the language of familial obligation and harmony. It is a kind of silent resistance against the unspoken demand for sexual conformity in the heterosexual family. Although some will accuse the strategy as a self-defeating compromise and a setback to the legitimate existence of the entire lesbian and gay community, I would attempt to discuss the new possibilities opened up by the cooperative marriage. In the following, I highlight two aspects of such possibilities: a new *tongzhi* space, and a new framework of family and marriage.

Cooperative marriages fully appropriate the logic of "a smile on the surface". It is a culturally specific strategy for *lalas* and gay people to survive in a culture where (heterosexual) marriage is not as much an option as an obligation to one's family and society, and a rite of passage to independence and adulthood. However, if we look at the productive side of cooperative marriages, we will discover that it not only nurtures new *tongzhi* counter-spaces, but also enables alternative ways of life and *tongzhi* household to take shape. Judith Halberstam's conceptualization of "queer temporality" suggests that queer space and time are not organized according to the heteronormative logic of life cycle which highlights marriage and reproduction (Halberstam 2005). By using the concept of "queer temporality", I do not suggest that there is a specific form of "queer life" in contemporary China that is distinctive from heteronormative ones. In fact, from what I have observed in my research, many *lalas*, regardless of their non-normative sexuality, aspire to lead a life that is temporally marked by a lifelong monogamous relationship and economic accomplishments. This resonates with the dominant heteronormative life narrative. What makes the idea of "queer temporality" useful here in my analysis is that it allows for a departure from conceiving cooperative marriage solely as a compromise to dominant norms. Instead, it directs our attention to the possible "opening up" of new life narratives, family forms, intimate alliances and *tongzhi* spaces. The cooperative marriage is not the ultimate result in the formation of queer time and space—if "queer" here refers to any practices and logic that challenge normative norms and order—on the contrary, it signals the beginning of the development of alternative forms of households, intimate alliances, kinship relationships, and life trajectories. On the surface, the heterosexual union in a cooperative marriage is the privileged relationship: The parties involved appear as a socially legitimate couple, and any same-sex connections to this heterosexual union are secondary. In reality, the marriage partners create for each other a new everyday space that accommodates their non-normative desires and relationships. This new space, which we can call a *tongzhi* counter-space, is no longer parasitic on the "formal" heterosexual marriage. The heterosexual marriage is more like a form without substance, while the same-sex relationships of both partners serve as the anchors of the entire performance. The introduction of a new *tongzhi* counter-space opens up further possibilities of family forms and kinship networks. The *tongzhi* households set up in a cooperative marriage can be further developed into an extended *tongzhi* kinship network, which now includes the two core marriage partners, their current same-sex partners, and other secondary kin members (as those *lalas* I met in my research connected with each other in kinship terms and stayed close as family members). It is a new form of family that is not connected by blood relation or conventional marital obligations. Thus, the nature of the relationships between kin members in a cooperative marriage can be highly contingent and negotiated. Although these new *tongzhi* households and spaces are invisible to the heterosexual public, they are indeed present, and are productive in the sense that they can not only accommodate the marriage partners' same-sex desires and practices, but can also function as valuable spaces for community development. These households are an essential community resource at a time when *tongzhi* are still struggling for spaces in both their private and social lives.

The cooperative marriage is a parody of the heterosexual marriage. It invites new insights into the institution of heterosexual marriage. The radical faking of the heterosexual law has an effect of displacing the divide of realness—which is always equated with heterosexuality—and illusion— which usually refers to homosexual practices. The disturbance that the cooperative marriage causes to the binaries of real and fake, object and shadow, primary and secondary, significant and insignificant, directs our attention to the very constructedness of this logic of division. It brings about a new line of enquiry that critically examines the symbolic order of normative and non-normative sexualities.

From the discussion above, the politics of public correctness is developed as a culturally specific resistance against the silent oppression enacted by the family institution in an era when the state is retreating from its direct influence on regulating citizens' private lives. It is necessary to understand contemporary forms of Chinese tolerance against sexually non-normative subjects as a force of homophobia in the first place, and to recognize the depoliticizing effect they accomplish by shaming "tolerated" subjects through the language of familial love and harmony. The ultimate aim is to maintain the heterosexual order and the surface harmony of the family. The politics also gives rise to the requirement of having to be a model member of society before one is qualified to exercise the act of coming out, thereby very likely intensifying an internal hierarchy of "good" and "bad", tolerable and intolerable homosexual subjects. Granting voice and visibility only to those homosexual subjects recognized by the repressive order, the logic of public correctness turns out to be a reinforcement of the repressive order. In other words, it in effect produces new repressive order of homonormativity.

The emergence of the cooperative marriage as the most elaborate form of the politics of public correctness indeed directs us to a new imagination of *tongzhi* space and existence. As Michael Warner says, "heteronormativity has a totalizing tendency that can only be overcome by actively imagining a necessarily and desirably queer world" (Warner 1991, p. 8). More attention needs to be paid to the productive aspects of cooperative marriage to *tongzhi* community and individual life options at a time when survival options are limited.

Conclusion: Seeing Diversity Among Us

The *tongzhi* communities in China are fast changing and internally diverse. The life stories, survival strategies and concerns of *lalas* included in this book represent mainly those of the group of *lala* informants whom I met in Shanghai during 2005–11. The discussion and analysis of *tongzhi* politics are based on my participation in the local *tongzhi* communities during the same period of time. My major site of research was Shanghai, but my participation in *tongzhi* activism in China allowed me to get in touch with local communities in other parts of the country. From the outset, this book did not aim to provide a generalization of *lala* lives in the post-reform era; rather, it was an attempt to document a portion of *lala* communities at a time when *tongzhi* movements are at a formative stage and when identity-based sexual and gender communities are just beginning to emerge in China. The conflict of the public and private lives of *lalas* was the central area of study. Research works on *lalas* in China are growing in number, but are still very limited compared to those on the gay communities in China. This study did not include groups of *lalas* who are "invisible", especially those who are not readily accessible in the present identity-based communities. For example, transgender identified *lalas*, women with same-sex desires who are from rural areas, who are economically and culturally deprived, or who are over fifty were not included. The informants of this study—mostly in their twenties and thirties, well-educated and of urban origin—represented the most active and visible group in the *lala* communities in Shanghai and other major cities in China during 2005–11. It is hoped that more documentation and studies of marginal groups of *lalas* can be carried out in the future.

The introduction of market economy and numerous social changes have dramatically transformed the most intimate lives of people in China. The "project *tongzhi*", as discussed in the Introduction, has attracted much attention from a global audience through its association with human rights and the pursuit of modernization; it has also attracted attention domestically with its role in the national campaign to build new discourses of sexual scientism. Paradoxical representations of *tongzhi* can be seen captured in the English and Chinese media in China, in the writings of different state experts and in the public remarks of local officials. Addressing the global audience, the state uses *tongzhi* to construct a new image of a democratic, modernized nation. Among domestic citizens, *tongzhi* is depoliticized as homosexuals, and is usually confined to the discussions of public health, security issues and academic studies. Media have shown a keen interest in the homosexual population in recent years. Individual *tongzhi* have appeared on popular television programmes and lifestyle magazines. Information about homosexuality is much more available to the general public. In 2011, it is estimated that there are hundreds of *tongzhi* websites in the country. They have been developing rapidly since the late 1990s with the help of new communication technologies such as the Internet, pagers and mobile phones. Individuals are easily connected into communities as a result, and this in turn, has led to the fast growth of local *lala* communities, particularly in the past decade. These communities were first formed on the Internet in forums and private chatrooms, and very soon, developed into independent *lala* websites. The three most popular *lala* websites in Shanghai were all launched in the first half of the 2000s. In 2005, the first official *lala* group made up of local women (with its core members from Shanghai and other parts of China), the *Nvai* Lesbian Group, was founded. In the years that followed, new *lala* groups emerged in different cities every year.

Emerging Diversities

As *tongzhi* communities in China are expanding and multiplying at great speed, internal diversities have emerged. In *lala* communities, minority groups such as married *lalas* first started to voice their specific concerns in as early as 2005. Debates surrounding norms of conduct, for example, forms of relationship, ethics of same-sex love, gender identifications and expressions have surfaced in *lala* communities. Transgender identified *lalas* and FTM (female-to-male transsexual people) are emerging and demanding visibility. Oral history projects are being carried out by local groups to track and document lives of *lala* women in old age, as well as women with same-sex desires but without explicit identifications. *Lalas* and gay men engaged in cooperative marriage are gathering together to provide mutual support, share experiences and exchange information. In 2011, a previously silenced group related to the male *tongzhi* population began to organize themselves and speak out in public. This group is made up of straight wives who are married to gay husbands. *Tongzhi* activists have been aware of their existence for some time, but it is only recently that this group has gathered in number and that their voices are beginning to be heard. Called *tongqi* in Chinese, meaning "the wives of *tongxinglian*", these self-empowered women have initiated many debates within the community.

The ongoing debate centres on the accusations by *tongqi* and the general public directed towards the gay population, and highlights the social and economic inequality between women and men in marriage and society as a whole. It is hoped that the circulation of the stories of *tongqi* would call into question the compulsory nature of heterosexual marriage in China. The impacts of *tongqi* and their emerging activism on *tongzhi* communities are yet to be evaluated.

At the time of writing, there is another ongoing debate within the *tongzhi* communities in China. The debate was sparked off by a discussion on whether it is suitable to apply queer theory to the *tongzhi* movements in China. The discussion first emerged in late 2011 on the micro-blog (*weibo*), one of the most popular social media platforms in China, between a group of anonymous *lalas* nicknamed "Sailor Moon Warriors" (*Meishaonü Zhanshi*) and a few well-known gay activists. It soon developed into a heated debate of queer theory versus "scientism", and constructivism versus essentialism of sexual orientation. The latter pair is usually expressed in terms of the dichotomy of nurture (*houtian*) versus nature (*xiantian*), which refers to the debate over the origins of homosexuality or sexual orientations in general. Some gay activists in China openly call for the condemnation of queer theory and dismiss efforts to introduce queer theory into the movement. The group of "Sailor Moon Warriors" then started a debate on *weibo* questioning the belief of homosexuality as inborn and introducing queer theory to the communities. It is estimated that their discussion has so far attracted thousands of followers on *weibo*. Many key members in the *tongzhi* communities in China have joined the debate. As the manuscript of this book was being finalized, this debate was only into its second week. Issues of diversity, internal hierarchization and male dominance of the *tongzhi* movements have been brought up. I foresee that it will herald a very important moment for the *tongzhi* movement in China. The debate is questioning the long-held dominance of scientific discourses in *tongzhi* communities, especially among the earlier developed male *tongzhi* groups. As discussed in Chapter 3, medical science has dominated the public discourse of homosexuality and sexuality in general for decades in China. It was also one of the inaugurative sites of the "modern homosexual"—the health conscious and self-empowered *tongzhi* in post-reform China. Many of the earlier male *tongzhi* groups were and still are funded by public health or science related grants. The influences of "scientism" are deep-rooted in China's *tongzhi* movement. Science or pseudo-scientific discourses are readily used by *tongzhi* activists to fight social prejudices. The pseudo-scientific belief of homosexuality as inborn and thus cannot be changed is widely adopted by some *tongzhi* activists to combat the general belief of homosexuality as a psychological or mental sickness, or a result of traumatic experiences. The idea of "queer", expressed as *qu'er* (酷兒) in Chinese, is not popular and well known in the *tongzhi* communities in China. Queer theory is only studied and discussed among the more educated groups of *lalas*, many of whom are university students and graduates. Queer theory, in this Internet debate, is interpreted as an extreme form of constructivism that promotes sexual fluidity. It is understood by the opposition as a dangerous discourse to the *tongzhi* movement in China, as they believe that ideas of constructivism are non-scientific and would be easily appropriated by conformists to impose aversion therapy on homosexuals, and hence would deprive *tongzhi* of a biologically legitimate position in society. I will not go into the details of this debate in this concluding chapter since analysis at this moment will be premature and ill informed. What I do want to highlight here is, from this ongoing debate, we can see that the *tongzhi* communities have reached a threshold at which internal differences are becoming visible. Those who are resourceless and marginalized are no longer silent, but are starting to speak up and challenge normative discourses in the communities. Within the *lala* communities, we can also hear the growing voices of younger groups in cities or regions where community development occurred much later than in major cities. Their voices represent newly developed groups and *lalas* living in economically less developed regions. The internal diversities call for a critical examination of existing homonormative discourses and power dynamics within the *tongzhi* communities.

Negotiating the Public and the Private

This book investigated how *lalas* cope with the new opportunities and new forms of social control of sexualities in China's post-reform period. Concerning the question of how new public discourses have affected the construction of a new *tongzhi* subjectivity, I argued that the new public inauguration of a self-affirmative *tongzhi* subjectivity has put *lalas* in a more difficult position of having to conform to heterosexual norms in their private lives while *lalas* generally hold aspirations to exclusive same-sex relationships independent of any heterosexual ones. The increasing public awareness of homosexuality also makes it less possible for *lalas* to pass as heterosexuals in their families and workplaces. The dilemma of the public and private is expressed most obviously through the pressure of marriage. Marriage was reported by all informants of this study as the major cause of stress in their everyday lives. For married informants, they have to cope with the pressures resulting from their marriages, natal families and their same-sex relationships. The institution of marriage has a tighter grip on women due to deep-rooted gender prejudices surrounding women's age, sexuality, social mobility and occupation in China. Women outside of heterosexual marriage are still stigmatized and understood as a less fortunate group. As an economically and socially inferior gender group, women's bargaining power in marriage is not as high as men's, as a result of which, the punitive effect of divorce is also more pronounced on women than on men. *Lalas* are doubly disadvantaged in the face of marriage. As women, they are culturally unrecognized as autonomous sexual subjects. This is evident in the absence of public discussion about female homosexuality, the under-representation of female *tongzhi* in the media (the term *"tongzhi"* has always equated to male *tongzhi*) and the popular belief of lesbian relationships as being sexless.

Strategies of coming out (*chugui*) are formulated according to the demands of filial piety and the close bonds between parents and children in Chinese families. Coming out is understood as a process of tactfully revealing one's sexuality to parents and to society. The strong familial control and intense day-to-day intimate surveillance of sexuality and the advocacy of state experts for "good" homosexuals (the presumed subject of homosexuality is always male) has generated culturally specific forms of resistance. This politics of public correctness, a response to the long history of state-imposed medical, moral and legal stigmatization of homosexual subjects, works to appropriate social norms to win homosexuals recognition from their families and the public. Even after the removal of "hooliganism" from the new Criminal Law and homosexuality from the newly revised list of mental illnesses, homosexuality continues to be understood as a threat to society and a psychological defect by the general public. *Tongzhi* communities prioritize destigmatization as the most urgent task at the moment. Images and notions of "healthy" and "sunny" *tongzhi* are circulated in the communities to refer to a form of *tongzhi* existence that diverges from the miserable and shadowy lives homosexuals have led in the past. Notions of "positive" or "proper" *tongzhi* are part of the state project to construct a new sexual morality for post-reform China, and to replace political struggles of sexual minorities with "class identity" and "culture" (Rofel 2007). As discussed in Chapter 5, cooperative marriage is a typical strategy informed by the politics of public correctness. It fully appropriates the surface order of the heterosexual family through an extreme performance of normative heterosexuality. I argued that cooperative marriage, even if it is a kind of conformity to heterosexual norms, also opens up new spaces for *tongzhi* existence and introduces new forms of family. It questions the naturalization of the heterosexual family and the normative connection of family with love. The households of cooperative marriage can also function as dispersed community spaces for *lalas* to gather. Cooperative marriage is widely regarded by *lalas* as a less than ideal solution. Its existence and popularity only highlight the intensity of the force of social conformity and the demands of what constitutes a "good" daughter, son and citizen in China. Despite the potential risks and shortcomings of cooperative marriage, I hope to direct our attention to the possible "opening-ups" of new life narratives, family forms, intimate alliances and *tongzhi* spaces.

Huang's Story

I would like to conclude this book by a story of a *lala* woman I met in 2005 in Shanghai. Huang was a newcomer to Shanghai when I first met her. She was in her late twenties, and had just run away from her family in a small city in South China. Her family had arranged a marriage for her after waiting for years in vain for her to get a boyfriend. She had lied to them that she was planning to stay in Shanghai for a few months to look for job opportunities. In fact, she was planning to stay as long as she could. Within months of arriving in the city, she happily joined the local *lala* community, and had started to share an apartment with a few new *lala* friends.

Huang had had a ten-year relationship with a woman in her hometown. As Huang's girlfriend got older, she began to face increasing pressure from her family to get married. Her family was incessant in arranging matchmaking meetings for her. They understood between them that if Huang did not like the man, Huang's girlfriend would respect her wishes and turn him down as well. Huang felt strongly that the male partner should at least be a person to whom she took some liking, before she would be willing to "hand over" her girlfriend. Huang accepted one of the men introduced to her girlfriend and agreed to let them date. She and her girlfriend put a hold on their relationship. Later, her girlfriend announced to Huang that she was getting married. Huang did not attend the wedding. After the wedding, Huang remained in touch, and became the godmother of her girlfriend's baby, who is named after Huang.

Huang and her girlfriend had tried to think of a solution. They had cried many times over it. Thinking back, Huang felt that her girlfriend was very brave. They had thought of running away, but there was nowhere to turn to. They believed that love would hold them together. At that time, they did not know any other people like them in their city.

Not long after, Huang faced pressure from her own family to get married. Her parents arranged dating opportunities for her time after time. One day, Huang heard firecrackers going off downstairs in front of her house. Her family had arranged a marital engagement between Huang and a young man whom she grew up with in her childhood. Acting according to their familial traditions, Huang's parents decided on October that year as the wedding date. Huang ran away to Shanghai in July. I came to know her in Shanghai in December the same year. By that time, she had already fled her marriage for more than five months. She had become a part of Shanghai's *lala* community, proudly identifying herself as a *T*.

Huang's story moves me deeply. I have also heard many similar ones from other *lalas* I met in different parts of China. All those stories show how one can take an active role to create a space for oneself, and how important community is to the individual *lalas*.

This book has attempted to document and discuss the life strategies of *lalas* who are living in Shanghai and other major cities in China. In the context of a fast-changing China, the rise of *tongzhi* communities is one of the most dramatic illustrations showing the significant transformations people's selves and intimate lives are undergoing, and how civil movements with diverse goals are informing each other to yield imaginings of new forms of democracy and possibilities in life. What kinds of *tongzhi* future can we imagine in China? I hope the lives and politics of *lalas* detailed in this book will propel readers on the journey of "seeing diversity among us".

Profiles of Key Informants

I conducted formal, semi-structured and recorded interviews with twenty-five informants from 2005 to 2010. Informants' personal information such as education, residence of natal family and occupation are altered for the sake of confidentiality. All names of key and supplementary informants quoted in this book are pseudonyms.

General Profile

The key informants of my research in Shanghai were self-identified *lala* women active in the *lala* communities in Shanghai. Their ages ranged from early twenties to mid-forties. All of them were ethnic Chinese and citizens of the People's Republic of China. All of them were urban residents. All but eight informants were not natives of Shanghai. At the time of interview, they were either working or studying in Shanghai. They were women who were in various degrees active within the local *lala* communities in Shanghai. Nearly all of them had white-collar jobs (or have had white-collar jobs but were studying for a second degree at the time of interview), or were self-employed. A few of them were staying in the city temporarily (for example, for study), and a few worked in nearby cities and came to Shanghai regularly either for home visits or social gatherings. Five of them were married, of whom two had children of their own. One of the five married informants was in a cooperative marriage with a gay partner. Two of the unmarried informants were planning cooperative marriages at the time of interview.

Individual Profiles

Bai, early twenties. Postgraduate education. A Shanghai native with an extended network of relatives in Shanghai. Not in marriage. Lived with her girlfriend. Had a white-collar job in a private firm and was a lesbian filmmaker. Took part in social gatherings of the local *lala* communities.

Chris, early thirties. University graduate. A Shanghai native with an extended network of relatives in Shanghai. Was planning a cooperative marriage. Lived with parents before marriage and would move in with her girlfriend after marriage. Had a white-collar job in a private firm. Took part in social gatherings of the local *lala* communities.

Coral, mid-thirties. Postgraduate education. Came from Northern China and had no family members in Shanghai. In a heterosexual marriage. Lived with her girlfriend and was enrolled in a postgraduate course in a local university. Husband knew she had extra-marital relationship but did not know it is a woman. Had private contact with *lala* friends in the local communities, but seldom participated in group gatherings.

Fish, mid-thirties. University graduate. A Shanghai native with an extended network of relatives in Shanghai. Not in marriage. Owned an apartment and lived with her girlfriend who was in a heterosexual marriage. A high-income professional. Had private contact with *lala* friends in the local communities, but seldom participated in group gatherings.

Grace, early thirties. University graduate. A Shanghai native. Not in marriage. Lived with her girlfriend. Self-employed. Had private contact with *lala* friends in the local communities, but seldom participated in group gatherings.

Heng, mid-thirties. Secondary education. A Shanghai native with an extended network of relatives in Shanghai. In a heterosexual marriage with a child. Lived with her husband and child. Had a girlfriend in another city. Husband and her had reached an agreement to open up their marriage and had extra-marital relationships. Self-employed. Had private contact with *lala* friends in the local communities, but seldom participated in group gatherings.

Jay, early thirties. University graduate. A Shanghai native. Not in marriage. Lived with her girlfriend. Self-employed. Had private contact with *lala* friends in the local communities, but seldom participated in group gatherings.

Jenny, mid-twenties. University graduate. A Shanghai native with an extended network of relatives in Shanghai. Not in marriage. Lived with parents. Was in a relationship with a local woman. A professional. Had private contact with *lala* friends in the local communities, but seldom participated in group gatherings.

Ling, late twenties. University graduate. A Shanghai native with an extended network of relatives in Shanghai. In a cooperative marriage. Lived with parents before marriage and with her long-term girlfriend after marriage. Had a white-collar job. Took part in social gatherings of the local *lala* communities.

Liu, early thirties. Post-secondary education. A Shanghai native with an extended network of relatives in Shanghai. Not in marriage. Had been in many relationships with women, and was currently single. Owned an apartment and lived on her own. A high-income professional. Had private contact with *lala* friends in the local communities, but seldom participated in group gatherings.

Long, mid-twenties. University graduate. Came from a city near Shanghai. Not in marriage. Was single for a period of time. Lived with relatives in Shanghai. Had a white-collar job. Took part in social gatherings of the local *lala* communities.

Matty, early twenties. University graduate. A Shanghai native with an extended network of relatives in Shanghai. Not in marriage. Lived with relatives. Was in a relationship with a woman, and was planning to emigrate from China together. A high-income professional. Rarely participated in the local *lala* communities.

May, mid-twenties. University graduate. Came from northern China and had relatives in Shanghai. Not in marriage. Lived on her own and later moved in with her girlfriend after her girlfriend had a cooperative marriage. A freelance writer and a volunteer for a local *lala* hotline.

Moon, early twenties. University graduate. A Shanghai native with an extended network of relatives in Shanghai. Not in marriage. Lived on her own with her girlfriend staying over regularly. Had a white-collar job at a private firm. An active member of the local *lala* communities and a host of a *lala* web radio in China.

Mu, mid-thirties. University graduate. A Shanghai native with an extended network of relatives in Shanghai. In a heterosexual marriage with a child and a long-term relationship with a woman in another country. Lived with husband and child and paid regular visits to her girlfriend. Husband knew she was having a relationship with a woman. A senior manager at a private firm. Took part in social gatherings of the local *lala* communities.

Qi, late twenties. Post-secondary education. Came from southern China and had no family members in Shanghai. Not in marriage. Lived on her own. Was in a long-distance relationship with a woman in another city. Worked as a self-employed web designer. An active member of the local *lala* communities.

Qing, late twenties. University graduate. A Shanghai native with an extended network of relatives in Shanghai. Not in marriage. Lived with relatives. Had been in a number of relationships with women and did not have a stable girlfriend. Had a white-collar job. Took part in social gatherings of the local *lala* communities.

Shu, mid-twenties. University graduate. Came from a city near Shanghai and had a few relatives in Shanghai. Not in marriage. Lived with her girlfriend. Had a white-collar job in a private firm. Took part in social gatherings of the local *lala* communities.

Sue, mid-forties. Secondary education. A Shanghai native. Not in marriage. Lived with her girlfriend. Had been in a number of relationship with women and had lived abroad for some years. Self-employed. Took part in social gatherings of the local *lala* communities.

Tan, late twenties. University graduate. A Shanghai native with an extended network of relatives in Shanghai. Was planning to have a cooperative marriage. Lived with her girlfriend who was in a cooperative marriage. A professional. Took part in social gatherings of the local *lala* communities.

Wei, mid-twenties. University graduate. A Shanghai native with an extended network of relatives in Shanghai. Not in marriage. Lived with her girlfriend. Had a white-collar job. Took part in social gatherings of the local *lala* communities.

Xiao, mid-twenties. University graduate. Came from western China and had no family members in Shanghai. Not in marriage. Lived with her girlfriend. Had a white-collar job in a private firm. Took part in social gatherings of the local *lala* communities.

Xu, mid-twenties. Secondary education. Came from northern China and had no family members in Shanghai. Not in marriage. Lived with her girlfriend. A lesbian party organizer who was well-known in the local *lala* communities.

Ya, early twenties. University graduate. A Shanghai native with an extended network of relatives in Shanghai. Not in marriage. Lived with her girlfriend. Had a white-collar job in a private firm. A volunteer for a *lala* hotline in Shanghai.

Ying, early thirties. University graduate. Came from northern China and had no family members in Shanghai. In a heterosexual marriage and had been in relationships with women before and after marriage. Was staying in Shanghai for study and also to take a break from marriage and family. Husband did not know she had girlfriends. Had private contact with *lala* friends in the local communities, but seldom participated in group gatherings.

Notes

Introduction

1. *"Lala"* has become a widely used term in the past five years, and its use can be traced back to the early 2000s. The term was adapted from the Taiwanese localization of "lesbian". It first appeared as *"lazi"* in Taiwan, as the transliteration of "les" from "lesbian". When it was borrowed and further localized in China, *"lala"* became the most widely used term. It is a community identity for women who have same-sex desires in China. It is used concurrently with *"tongzhi"*, an older and Hong Kong-derived identity, in its full or gender-specific versions such as *"nütong"* (female *tongzhi*) and *"nantong"* (male *tongzhi*); and with "les", an abbreviation and a more informal term for "lesbian". There are contextual differences between various identity terms. *"Lala"* and "les" are always used in informal or everyday and lesbian-specific contexts, while *"tongzhi"* is used in more formal and political occasions where community solidarity is emphasized. All identities are generally recognized and adopted in local communities across the country. In this book, I use *"lala"* to refer to lesbian, bisexual and transgender identified women, and *"tongzhi"* when I refer to entire LGBTQ communities in China. I use "lesbian" and "gay" when I do not refer to any specific cultural or geographical context.

2. A cooperative marriage is a self-arranged marriage between a *lala* woman and a gay man. It is performed to deal with the marriage pressure imposed by families on both sides.

3. An Internet survey conducted by a local news website in China found that over 70% of respondents (3,977 in total) said they can accept if their children are homosexuals (quoted from www.cctv.com on 6 November 2007).

4. The oral history project mentioned is "Hong Kong Women-Love-Women Oral History Project" (2005), which resulted in the publication of a collection of life stories of women in Hong Kong who have same-sex desires.

5. Lucetta Y. L. Kam (editor and illustrator). *Lunar Desires: Her first same-sex love in her own words* (月亮的騷動──她她的初戀故事：我們的自述) (Hong Kong: Cultural Act Up, 2001).

Chapter 1

1. 「拉子一詞，傳到香港又傳到大陸中國後，演變成拉拉。在現在的大陸中國，就出現了一些拉拉網站、拉拉驛站、拉拉酒吧和拉拉社區等各種各樣的女同性戀的組織和

活動形式。因此，拉拉這個詞語的出現，不僅使女同性戀者得以去做身份認同，也
使得她們能夠利用這一身份，去創建自己的社區，去團結和發現更多的拉拉們來開
展活動和組織活動。」

2. Wang Hui (2003) argues that neoliberalism in China has its own context of develop-
    ment and relationship with the state. The force of market in China is less a resist-
    ance from the people than part of a state promoted displacement of social problems.
    "While neoliberalism takes every opportunity to cast itself in the image of 'resister',
    this does not prove that this ideology of the market is in actual opposition to the
    practical operations of the state: on the contrary, the state and neoliberalism exist
    in a complex relationship of codependence" (p. 60). Dai Jinua (2006) also argues
    that the economic restructuring of China uses the rhetoric of market to displace
    emerging social inequalities brought about by the changes. Gender inequality has
    been displaced by class discourse. Uneven distribution of wealth is justified by
    development. The state has engaged ideologically in the construction of the new
    discourse of market and neoliberalism.

3. Two of the novels that have been circulated widely in Shanghai *lala* communities
    are Zhang Haoying's *Shanghai Wangshi* (上海往事, *The Bygone Story of Shanghai*)
    published by Guangxi Renmin Chubanshe in 2003 and Hailan's *Wode Tianshi Wode
    Ai* (我的天使我的愛, *My Angel My Love*) published by Zhongguo Xijue Chubanshe
    in 2007.

4. *T* is the masculine identified lesbian gender in China. It is an adoption of the lesbian
    gender identity in Taiwan, where *T* is classified as the masculine role and *P* (or *Po*)
    is the feminine role.

5. 「國內除了上海這樣的大城市，一些小的城市，甚至是一些小的鄉鎮，就是一個紅綠
    燈也沒有的那種鄉鎮，更小的是在農村裡面，她們根本就沒有機會得到很多的資
    訊。我只有在這個網絡發達的時候，我才能夠……我沒有得到這個資訊的時候，我
    已經二十幾歲了，我要談男朋友了，我在讀書的時候我也跟我的……同學有過親密
    的接觸，我們都不覺得這是什麼，也沒有人……不可能有人告訴我們，我又不會去
    問別人，也沒有書籍，也沒有網絡，不知道是什麼。然後……我們就覺得這只不過
    是一個過程，那到了時候我就應該去談戀愛，然後去交男朋友，去準備結婚，就這
    樣了。一直到我……我覺得我很幸運的是我跟我男朋友分手，然後我知道了網絡。
    我一直是覺得很幸運的，不然我肯定要嫁給他了。你想想如果我嫁給他，到我上了
    網，到了網上才確認自己，我回想我以前跟我同學的事，那我不會覺得很苦嗎？所
    以我覺得這個資訊溝通很重要的。」

6. The "2005 China Internet Usage Survey Report" conducted by the Chinese Academy
    of Social Sciences in five cities in China (Beijing, Shanghai, Guangzhou, Chengdu
    and Changsha), quoted from Liu Huaqing (2005) *Tianya Virtual Community: Text-
    based Social Interactions on the Internet* (天涯虛擬社區：互聯網上基於文本的社會互動
    研究) (Beijing: Minzu Chubanshe), pp. 33–34.

7. There are different views in the community regarding why the lesbian nights were
    cancelled in 2003. Some say it was due to their popularity and alarming attendance.
    On a typical weekend evening, Bar 1088 attracted more than three hundred custom-
    ers. One woman even told me she was there at one of the crowded weekend parties
    when the police suddenly appeared and ended the party. Women were asked to
    line up for inspection. The police claimed illegal drug use in the party had been
    reported. But the woman said the police gave them no trouble, and had released
    the party-goers all at once. Others said there had not been any police crackdowns or

interventions, and that the lesbian party organizers had left because of a disagreement with the bar owner.

Chapter 2

1. 「同性戀是不是病呢？那可不能簡單地作結論。我們只能說同性戀者的性心理是不正常的。因為正常人的性心理活動的指向，總是異性，也就是所謂『窈窕淑女，君子好逑』。而同性戀者的性心理指向，所愛慕的對象卻是同一性別的，這是一種性心理方面的變態。但是，為什麼造成性心理的改變呢？這裡可能有生理、心理和社會三個方面的因素……如果發現同性戀患者的主要原因是生理改變，應作為『疾病』來對待，並給以適當的治療……從變態心理學角度分析，同性戀的戀人中，性心理反常者，主要是女性『丈夫』，和男性『妻子』……所以，他們可能是需要接受治療或心理指導的對象，因為他們心理學上的性定向是不正常的。」

2. 「同性戀是不符合生物本性的。從生物學的觀點來看，人類的性行為是與生殖聯繫在一起的。同性是不能生育的。同性戀在人群中的擴展，將導致種族繁衍上的嚴重問題。但是，也不能因為同性戀不生育而蔑視以至懲罰同性戀者。有相當一部份異性夫婦（其數量不少於同性戀者）是不育的，社會並不因此而責難他們；在計劃生育的時代，絕大部份性行為也是與生殖無關的，社會不僅不責難，反而要提倡這一點。為什麼同性戀就要因為不育而受罪責呢？」

3. 「當然，這裡並不是提倡同性戀。確實看不出同性戀有什麼好處。而且同性戀者面臨著一系列社會的、道德的、法律的、經濟的、疾病的壓力，有種種後果。因此，根本不值得提倡。事實上也提倡不了，沒有辦法把一個『絕對異性戀者』變為同性戀者。正像沒有辦法把一個『絕對同性戀者』變為異性戀者一樣。即使對同性戀者處以死刑的國家、民族或宗教裡，也沒有能夠根絕同性戀。這裡所要強調的只是：應該正視同性戀問題，並合理對待它。」

4. 「對於同性戀，也是『預防為主』。家庭的和諧；對兒童進行良好的教育，包括及時而適當的性教育；創造青少年之間異性交往的文明環境和條件等等，可能都有助於減少同性戀的出現。」

5. Evans also mentions this narrative incoherence in experts' writings on homosexuality in post-reform China, "Other observations about homosexuality reveal a similar tension, between sympathetic demands for tolerance and recognition on the one hand, and a persistent attachment to the view of homosexuality as a deviant or diseased state on the other. Liberal scholars working on sex education and other sex-related issues continue to present homosexuality as a sickness, despite their demands for recognition of homosexuals' rights" (Evans, 1997, p. 209).

6. 「切實認識它的起因和意義，透徹地明白它可能存有的危害，用科學的方法積極進行預防和處理。」

7. 「同性愛現象研究史」，「同性愛的定義、流行狀況和分型」，「同性愛的表現」，「同性愛的起因」，「同性愛與心理（精神）疾病的關係」，「同性愛的預防與治療」，「與同性愛（性行為）有關的性偏離」，「同性愛者與性有關的器質性疾病」，「同性愛與性道德」，「同性愛與性法律」。

8. 「同性愛是一個社會深層的性苦難和性悲劇。」

9. 「以期改變我國目前學術界，特別是醫學界對這一常見社會現象的知識匱乏、認識膚淺的現狀，並幫助廣大讀者澄清這一現代的性誤區；幫助異性愛大眾科學地認識與對待同性愛者，並幫助同性愛患者增強自我規範的力量。」

10. 「我在部隊因同性睡覺，受過黨內警告處分，當時把我當做雞姦錯誤。1968至1978年間，也把我當做雞姦錯誤處理，直到判刑……我要求到醫院檢查，由於單位的態度，不准我去檢查，後來我還是偷偷地到xx醫學院檢查，才知道是同性戀。然後又經北京三所醫院檢查，確診為同性戀。1980年省高等法院糾正錯判後，才恢復工作，但至今卡住黨籍和錯處期工資未補發。」

11. 「被告xxx因流氓罪一案，判處有期徒刑二年監外執行，後改判免予刑事處分。現經再次複查：原判認定事實不構成犯罪。因xxx患有『同性戀』病。為此，撤銷原判和複查改判的判決，予以糾正。」

12. 「在這場討論中，艾滋病的傳播本身就成了一種文化工具。國家用它來擴大對私人生活的干預；並且，對於宣傳冊的讀者來說，這個意義遠遠超過預防艾滋病。這是由警察和其他權力機構對同性戀者的騷擾和拘禁，以及執法機關和公共衛生機構對同性戀者根深蒂固的不信任所造成的。」

13. For example, Article 19 Section 4 of the "Regulations Governing Offences Against Public Order" issued in 1994 states that, "inciting gang activities or violence, behaving in a riotous or disorderly manner, or insults at women or other forms of hooliganism"（結伙鬥毆，尋釁滋事，侮辱婦女或者進行其他流氓活動的），the content of "hooliganism" can be open to arbitrary interpretations. [Information source: Jia Ping (2005) *Report of rights, legal problems and related issues of homosexual (bisexual) in China* (同（雙）性戀相關法律問題綜述)] (Beijing: Aizhixing Institute of Health Education), p. 12.

14. 「如杭州一市1988年一年左右，司法機關即拘捕男性同性愛者60人以上。拘捕須判刑的主要依據是刑法第160條。該條文規定：『聚眾鬥毆、破壞公共秩序，情節惡劣的，處7年以下有期徒刑、拘役或管制。流氓集團的首要分子，處7年以上有期徒刑。』」

15. 「我國司法機關1987年曾就同性愛的法律地位所做的申明：『由於同性愛違反社會公德，擾亂社會治安，影響青少年身心健康，確屬犯罪行為。』」

16. Quoted from *Huakaidedifang*, http://www.lescn.net/, on 15 December 2005.

17. 「什麼是同性戀，以及同性戀的責任問題在目前我國法律沒有明文規定的情況下，你們所反映的問題，原則上可不予受理，也不宜以流氓行為給予治安處罰。本案具體如何處理，可與檢察院、法院等有關部門研究解決。」

18. Evans criticizes the research, asserting that "it represents homosexuality as a 'phenomenon' distanced from dominant heterosexual culture and objectified for the purposes of study" (Evans 1997, p. 209).

19. 「那個聊天室，當然是男同、女同都有，而且年紀比較小。進去了，剛開始的時候在看，看她們在聊，然後就很好奇，原來有這麼多人跟自己有類似的經歷。但是沒想到是這樣的，是同性戀，我就很排斥這樣，就不會……我跟她們是不一樣的。但事實上，你看到的越多，你就驗證的越多，你就知道你就是其中的一個人。再後來，慢慢的到語音的聊天室啊，然後到一些網站去看，然後你一邊看，一邊找自己身上跟她們相認證的東西。」

20. 「我在百度搜了『女同』兩個字，然後上了之後，跳出來了一個網站，和一些學術的報告，我沒有選擇看網站，而是看了些學術的報告，一些教授和一些很學術的文章，非常的寬泛的說了女同，在女同的世界裡，分為T、P和不分等等這些的概念。一下子就在我的腦海裡，於是我和她的關係就copy進去，也明確了許多的概念。隨後進了一些網站，我第一個進入的是叫『夢開始的地方』，是一個不是很成熟的網站，但是也聚集了許多的les，於是看了一篇女同文章，是關於女同之間做愛的，然後我就明白了女同之間是怎麼做愛的，什麼口交和手指，我也是很籠統的我也不懂。後來認識了一個女同，帶我進入了一個聊天室，她當時是某女同性網站的管理員，因為她我就進了那個房間。一進去就發現，哇嗦，裡面全都是les，就覺得有那麼多，我並不孤單，原來我不是異類，原來有那麼那麼多！」

21. 「我第一個感覺就是說，你會覺得你自己的戀愛的過程是獨一無二，你的經歷對你來說是最重要的。但是你到網上去看很多帖子的時候，忽然發現很多是類似的。因為暗戀一個人是每個人幾乎都有的過程，無法表白。哎呀，你會發現這麼火！你在網上你會發現很多人都是這樣子的。這就是說，第一個反應就是，你不是唯一的，你們是一體的；然後第二個就是，她們會發出一些她們想見面啊，徵友啊這樣的資訊。這種資訊發出來了後，你覺得很正常，覺得大家可以相互之間見面的。然後這個跟你平時看到的這個人沒有太大的區別啊，大家都這樣生活得不錯啊。第三個，你們一起聊共同的想法以及未來的時候啊，你覺得……像我去北京的話，我就覺得，哦，你十多歲也能這樣，那我的未來遠景是不錯的。她們讓我看到了希望。那你以前不會去想，因為你覺得不現實，你看不到這樣的例子，或者是怎麼樣。但是看到她們的時候，就是有未來。」

Chapter 3

1. 「打開一個衣櫃啊，一半是我的衣服，一半是她的，每個晚上她都在我的身邊，沒有一個晚上是我自己度過的。〔可現實是〕我一個人上網。遇到不開心的事，我會自己一個人哭。我希望我的生活裡都有她的氣息。這個家是兩個人的家，而不光只有我自己的東西。我希望她徹徹底底的成為我生活的一部分。」

2. Evans (1997) explains very well the effect of this discursive hegemony on Chinese women, "The priority the dominant discourse gives to maintaining monogamous marriage as the site and pivot of all sexual activity and experience is overriding. This leaves no discursive space for women—or men—to choose difference, whether this means simply not marrying, having a lover outside marriage, or rejecting heterosexuality. In fact, it leaves no alternatives for representations of a women's sexual fulfillment except in the subject positions identified by the status of wife and mother. The possibility that women may prefer to live separate lives, removed from the dominance of the male drive, cannot be contained within a discourse which naturalizes monogamous marriage as the only legitimate form of adult existence" (p. 212).

3. Comparing with other Chinese societies, the figure for the unmarried population aged 15 or over in Hong Kong was 31.5% in 1996 and 31.9% in 2001 (Census and Statistics Department, Hong Kong Special Administrative Region 2005), and 34.1% in Taiwan in 2004 (National Statistics 2005).

4. 「因為婚姻不是一場簡單的戀愛，你會考慮很多東西，家庭啊、社會啊。因為一個人的婚姻情況會關係到她的社會。因為有時候會因為你的婚姻關係會影響到其他本來看是不相干的事情，也可能這會是給了別人攻擊你的把柄，你的父母會擔心。」

5. 「沒有想過這是一條路，就是覺得每個人都應該結婚……沒有這樣參照的例子啊，覺得每個人都應該走這樣的路。可能那個時候想的最多的是自己比較特殊吧，你的特殊不能破壞社會正常的秩序，你還是要負責任的，對家人、對父母負責。包括自己的狀態，你都不見的有那樣的能力去挑戰，況且兩個人都沒有想過，好像就已經不是問題，就覺得這不應該是考慮的問題，根本沒有考慮的可能性。」

6. 「那時候很怕別人提到這三個字，因為我跟我那個女朋友在一起的時候有朋友會開玩笑說你們兩個好的像同性戀一樣，我們兩個就會一起反擊。因為首先對自己就是一種不認可，其實到現在看來就是對自己這種行為的不認可，所以才會去反擊。不過如果說我們兩個人從剛開始就接觸到了這樣一個環境，就說會有人給你一種方向吧。那個時候我們兩個在一起自己都不知道該怎樣辦，經常都會撥了電話以後就兩個人一起哭，說以後該怎麼辦，就是沒有什麼東西讓你參照。如果我想如果那個時候我們上網可能會在一起，會在一起……衝破很多東西。你根本不會去想你可以過這樣的一種生活，覺得沒有將來，覺得沒有人走這樣一條路，沒有想過這是一條路，覺得每個人都應該結婚……我記得我在結婚前的一個晚上，是她陪我在外面，家裡去了很多的親戚，剛好就找了一個理由說，這樣休息不好，就她陪我去外面開房間住在那邊，第二天早上回去化妝啊，做一些準備，真的是……兩個人整整的一直在那裡哭，哭到零晨四點鐘，我結婚的前一天。」

7. 「你沒有婚姻吧，沒有婚姻的人不會知道把婚姻挑到肩膀上的時候，意味著什麼。我就是這樣簡單的跟你講，就是責任，你就會覺得說什麼是責任，你會覺得很抽象。實際上婚姻並不是兩個人的事情，會牽涉到兩個人之外很大的一群人，家族，甚至朋友，甚至同事，你不會懂，沒有婚姻的人你真的不會懂。你也許會理解我，或者是同情我，但是很多感覺，你也是感受不到。」

8. 「我不會去傷害人家，但我也不想去傷害自己，所以即使說找不到一份你很有感覺的感情，哪怕是單身也無所謂。但是我覺得這是比較有壓力，因為對家庭來說，或者對身邊人來說，他們是很不能夠接受的。他們當然覺得隨便怎樣你當然是應該有婚姻、有好的歸宿、有家庭這樣，但我跟他們說，像我也不太適合家庭生活，因為我覺得我是一個比較喜歡自由的人，不希望被人來束縛我這樣子。我曾經說過，當然我沒有對我父母說過我要單身，因為我覺得他們是絕對不能夠接受的。我曾經跟我同事跟朋友說過我要單身，他們就一下子都跳起來了，『那怎麼可以啊？！』，隨後他們就馬上說，『你不應該有這種想法』。」

9. 「一般獨身的女孩子給人的感覺蠻不幸的，為什麼？哪怕她是女強人，總是覺得她的感情生活不如意。否則的話，如果能找到一個疼愛她的男人，哪怕是女人也好，她肯定不會選擇一個人過。她獨身，是因為她沒有找到一段符合要求、很美好很和諧的感情。只要她有好的感情，為什麼會獨身？哪怕是女強人，再工作狂也不會這樣。還是輿論的力量，他們覺得他們的孩子自己一個人，外面人各種各樣的原因，承受的猜疑壓力還是受不了的……還有很多時候，你不結婚，永遠是被關心的對象。有人跟你說，你女兒還沒結婚？還是沒有男朋友嗎？或者是怎麼樣。只要你不結婚，你永遠是被關心的對象。如果你結婚了，出嫁了，就沒人理你。」

10. There is a park in downtown Shanghai where a Saturday matchmaking event is held once a month. It attracts many parents who are looking for suitable mates for their adult children. Regular participants of the event will hold a cardboard on which is written the information of the person who is seeking a partner. Parents will usually carry the cardboard bearing information about their child and also the kind of partner they expect for their children. Parents will exchange contact numbers if they are interested, and both sides will proceed to arrange meetings for their children if they are interested in seeing each other.

11. 「因為他們覺得沒有面子哦。如果你結婚就不是我家的常屬人員，不會被關心這麼多了，就是照顧一下他們的面子了。」

12. 「因為我覺得徹徹底底擺脫家裡，唯一的方法就是自己出來住，自己買房子。因為你出來租房子，父母肯定是不能接受，除非我自己出來買房子，這點沒有話可說。所以這兩個壓力結合在一起，如果我在家裡沒有任何的壓力的話，我買房子的欲望就沒有那麼的強烈，但是一定會的，因為不可能是想跟她一起就一直的租房子住，我覺得很缺乏安全感的，一定會自己買房子。但是對家裡的壓力，在自己的時間表裡就要求得更短了，本來我可以時間長一些，可能是五年或者是十年的時間。」

13. *Bufen* is a lesbian gender and sexual identification in local *lala* communities. It refers to *lalas* with an androgynous gender presentation or *lalas* who refuse to label themselves as either *T* or *P*. *Bufen* usually claims to have a more fluid desire that is not limited towards either *T* or *P*.

14. 「所以如果我一直不交男朋友，打扮過於中性的話，她會懷疑，甚至會直接了當的問我，你究竟是不是？〔問過？〕問過，但是我沒有正面回答，她也沒有正面追問下去。有時候人會有一種敏感度，很多東西不能過於執著。〔你從小都是比較中性的嗎？〕對，但是也有時候是非常女性化打扮的，並不是那種所謂的純T或者純P，我是不分這種。〔但你媽媽現在還是懷疑？〕有一點懷疑，但是我這兩年打扮得女性化比較多，也穿裙子，也留過長髮，拍過照片給她作為存檔証據給她看（笑）〔比較放心了？〕對，她心裡就安慰很多。真的很明顯，因為她也是一種很情緒化的很孩子氣的，很明顯的就能看得出我某一天穿襯衫剪短髮，她會很不高興，但是某一天如果我穿了裙子高跟鞋，昂首挺胸的走的話，留著長髮，她會樂不可支。她覺得『唔，這兩天比較正常，那個時候肯定是不正常的』。（笑）」

15. 「參加她們家的所有活動，這是不可能的呀！我可以到她的家吃飯，然後我可以睡在她的家裡，我可以陪她，甚至可以看看電視，有時候聊一下，就這樣吧，不可能參加公眾的活動，這是不可能的。如果看到了她媽媽的朋友的話，她會說是她姐姐的女兒，外甥女，等於是替我們來撒謊。我不能孤立在她們家之外，肯定不會，我會經常去她的家裡，我會經常被人看到，很不容易。」

Chapter 4

1. 「好像天天被兩種的力量不停的轉啊，轉啊，就是這樣一直轉下去。」

2. 「雖然說 come out 是一個非常值得欽佩的一種行為嘛，但是必須去看具體情況而定的，不是說你去做勇士了。〔你接熱線的時候也會這樣說嗎？〕對，我會這樣跟她說，我不鼓勵出櫃，這是一個需要慎重而慎重考慮的事情，特別是……你的條件允不允許你出櫃，很現實的，我會非常的……就是赤裸裸的告訴她們的，你（長音）出櫃得起嗎？」

3. "Super Girls" (or "Super Voice Girls") is a televised singing contest for young women in China, produced and broadcast by the Hunan Satellite Television, following the style of American Idol. The show was launched in 2004, and soon became a nationwide hit. Super Girls finalists were followed by crowds of fans from all over the country. A few of them became lesbian icons for the younger generation. The most famous are Li Yuchun and Zhou Bichang. Their androgynous style resembles the T style in the *lala* community. They have attracted millions of *lala* and straight women fans from diverse age groups.

4. 「我媽媽也很喜歡她們兩個人，然後就傳她們是一對啊，我媽媽也知道。我也跟我媽媽說，而且其他的娛樂的新聞也說，李宇春跟一些女孩子接吻啊什麼的一些照片，我媽也看見了，我媽也就一直也很喜歡她。我突然就覺得這個契機快來了，我媽知道這麼多關於李宇春和何潔的同性戀啊，尤其是李宇春啊這些負面的報導，我媽沒有絲毫減少對她的喜歡，而且我媽還介紹那些阿姨、同事，介紹她們一起去喜歡李宇春。有一次，決賽的時候，是『超級女聲』，我媽看得很緊張，而且很開心很興奮，於是我問媽，你這麼的喜歡李宇春啊，她滔滔不絕的說了大堆喜歡李宇春的原因，她還說她哭，就是李宇春哭，她也哭，『那你知不知道李宇春是喜歡女孩子的？』『這沒有關係的啦，她這麼的男孩子，我也想得到的啦！』然後，我就說，『你相不相信她喜歡過我？』我媽就看看我說，『你們是同一個大學的，而且同屆的，不可能的。』『是我拒絕了她。』，我媽很失望的說，『你幹什麼拒絕她？』然後我就笑笑說，『哎呀，你看電視吧！』〔……〕我說像李宇春的這些女孩子在這個城市，在這個國家，在這個世界，是非常非常得多的，嗯，也許很多人不理解，但是中國有幾千萬，而且我生活的城市有很多，我們的學校更多。」

5. Flora was a supplementary informant in addition to the twenty-five primary ones.

6. 「當時我看到我爸爸媽媽也蠻難受的。我記得最清楚的一次是,我在他們那邊養了一星期的病。每次他們要吃飯的時候,就把門輕輕推開,進來看看我是在睡覺還是怎麼樣,總問我要吃什麼怎麼樣。很難受,自己吃不下,可是為了他們又裝出來自己想吃什麼。後來實在受不了,這樣養下去也把我爸爸媽媽折磨,太操心了。有一天下午,我就突然從床上坐起來,說我要回家,那時候身體其實很虛弱,後來我爸媽就執意不肯。北方的十一月份已經很冷了,因為我去的時候也沒有穿很厚的衣服,那我就披了一件外套。就是我就講了一下我要回家,也沒有跟他們商量一下,也不會聽他們意見。我穿了外套,就拉開房門我就出去了。我媽媽就一直喊我說你這樣不能回去啊,回去也沒有人照顧到你。看我執意要走,就匆匆忙忙跑進去要幫我拿外套,但是我不知道,當時我就衝出去了。等我坐到一輛出租車裡,我走得很快,頂著風,有點像小跑那樣。我坐到出租車裡一扭頭,看到我媽媽拿著一件外套在那裡追我。那個情景可能我一輩子都忘不了。所以我就想之後我要選擇這樣的生活絕對不要在他們的面前⋯⋯我可能永遠不會主動的去出櫃,不是說我不能去面對什麼,是我覺得如果這種東西,如果讓周圍愛你的人受到傷害,那大可不必。能避免的東西還是去避免,對嗎?別的人倒沒什麼,但父母⋯⋯永遠不能對他們說為了你自己把他們置於一個不管不顧的地步。我想我曾經已經這樣做過了,以後會盡量避開。」

7. Huang was a supplementary informant in addition to the twenty-five primary ones.

8. 「其實爸爸媽媽總是希望你自己開心的,我覺得他們的問題是在面子上過不去。這裡很多親戚啊朋友啊什麼的,所以我覺得真的出去了也有好處,他們說起來她一個人在外面不想結婚。他們看不到你,就算你告訴了他們,他們沒有必要跟別人說。他們其實是⋯⋯就好像有一次我爸爸跟我說,像你這樣子在中國是沒有辦法做的,他就這麼跟我說。他說這個國家還沒有這麼開放,你這樣做⋯⋯你以後工作啊什麼的你沒有辦法抬起頭來。」

9. 「雖然有些人說我們之間的戀愛跟別人是沒有關係,但是至少不要給周遭的人帶來非常大的壓力,或者是非常大的影響。你的事情不要影響到別人的生活⋯⋯我覺得他們沒辦法理解。家裡的話,能不講就不講。講出來還是會鬧,那就沒必要。等到有一天真的沒辦法,那麼,就公開了。但是我至少覺得⋯⋯到現在為止,能藏就藏吧,不要去講,講了一定會是不好的狀況。」

10. 「那現在我既然走的是拉拉這條路,那我想這正好就是一個重合點啦。首先我是拉拉,第二我是獨身主義,那我肯定是雙重的否定不會去結婚。我會以各種各樣的方式來向父母證明我這樣活得很好,〔獨身?〕對。就是從我的事業,從我的朋友圈,從我的生活的質量,來告訴他們。我覺得事實勝於雄辯,至少不能說我這樣就好到一個什麼程度,但我至少不比我同齡的結婚的那些差,對吧?」

11. 「我想過這個問題,什麼樣的狀態對我來說比較的好。就是第一個,家裡的人覺得這個人對你很好,第二個就是家裡的人能夠接受她,因為作為你的女朋友絕對是對你好不會對你壞的,還有你們兩個必須要有一定物質的基礎,不會說兩個人在一起生活都成為問題了,那這樣的話家裡人也是很難接受,肯定是我們在一起過了很長的時間,過了兩至三年,甚至是更久了之後,她們是覺得你們在一起很正常,而且她非常的照顧你,家裡人看不到她覺得少了什麼東西,很重要的時候,那我覺得可以慢慢得跟他們說這些的狀況,而現在還是太早啦。」

12. 「我不知道兩個女人走下去最大的困難是什麼,但是我知道,如果要讓兩個女人一直走下去,最大的保障是什麼,是經濟,有足夠的經濟才能更大的保障你們可以走下去⋯⋯跟一個女人在一起,即使你們的經濟基礎很有保障的話,也會有重重的困難;而跟一個男人在一起的話,即使你們的經濟不是很好,但是其他的都不成問題,就是只看兩個人的感情的問題啊。」

13. 「我記得我上網的認識的第一個朋友,她跟我說的一句話,她說,『這個世界上無論怎樣的一種的愛情,都需要物質基礎的,尤其是這樣的一種的愛情,因為你得不到任何的援助。你是孤立無援的,如果你再不能為自己支撐起來一些東西,那是很難在一起。』這話可能太現實了,其實是事實是這樣,有多少沒有條件的愛情,不太可能。」

14. 「我覺得雖然相親是件很可笑的事情,也很嫌他們很多事很雞婆。但是你換個角度去想,他們正因為是你的親人,是你的朋友,他們會關心你去做這個。假如你到了這個年紀,沒有任何人關心你是否有男朋友或女朋友在你身邊,沒有人在意你是一個人兩個人,沒有人去想過你是不是需要一個伴侶,那這個人真的是太可怕了。我覺得這反而是讓我恐慌的事情。」

15. 「但是因為當時我已經想到最最徹底的方法就是啊……不怪怎麼樣講至少人家鑾好的,結婚就結婚吧,即使不好就離婚囉。那麼對我來說,我已經沒壓力了,反正我已結過婚了,那麼離婚和之後的事情,就用不著再說了吧。」

16. 「開始了一年以內丈夫知道……我現在是覺得有婚姻的女人不要……去愛另一個女人,如果我是三年前知道是這個狀況,儘管我很愛她,我一定會控制的,因為這樣的話你害的是三個人,三個人都痛苦的。如果我可以知道是今天這個場面的話,我寧可在當天小痛一下,真的是很害人的……現在她很痛苦,她一直覺得沒有安全感,我給不了她安全感,又不能給承諾。然後婚姻那邊先生他也很痛苦,因為正常的男人可以擁有的一切我也給不了他。我自己也非常痛苦,有的時候就想過很簡單的生活,每天早上睜開眼睛感到沒有任何的壓力,簡簡單單的笑一下,工作、看看書。現在每天早上醒來一睜開眼睛覺得心裏很多東西壓著,很沉的……那個時候我很想離婚的,我跟他都談過離婚的,他的態度就是沒有關係,你不用擔心,你去做你想做的,沒有關係的,不用考慮我,我就在這邊,一直在,你願意回來就回來。他如果不是這種寬容的態度,也許我離婚的決心就更大了。當時他那種態度讓我沒辦法。」

17. For example, the divorced population (aged 15 or over) in China in 2004 was only 1.07% (China Statistics Press 2005), while it was 5.2% in Taiwan in 2004 (National Statistics 2005b) and 2.7% in Hong Kong in 2001 (Census and Statistics Department, Hong Kong Special Administrative Region 2005).

18. 「他的反應?就覺得出乎意料。然後就覺得他的人生可以寫個故事了,怎麼會有這樣的事情發生在他身上?但是既然已經發生了,再說對象也是個女的嘛,對他來說不是男性的話對他不會有那麼大的威脅,而且又隔得那麼遠,也就接受了。男的肯定不接受,她的丈夫也一樣,覺得你們兩個女的反正也做不成什麼事情嘛,(笑)。但是一開始她老公那邊也覺得很……很生氣,怎麼有外遇了,後來知道是個女的,就慢慢、慢慢的接受了。」

19. 「孩子是相當大的因素,因為沒有孩子的話,兩個人離婚就離婚了,也就無所謂,經濟上大家分隔一下就好了。有了孩子的話,這對孩子的影響非常大,這絕對不能夠太自私為了自己的幸福來把孩子將來的人生或幸福給破壞掉了。一部份是經濟,還有小孩子個人會受到打擊,會受到影響,所以說對孩子的成長、健康不是很有利,不能為了自己的快樂而影響到孩子的未來嘛。這是一個很重要的考慮因素。還有當然還有經濟方面的因素,如果說經濟上面不成熟的話,兩個人待在一起將來很可能還是好不了的,因為會有磨擦嘛,那磨擦了以後就會分手。如果說花了驚天動地的力量待在一起,結果還是分手的話,那就代價太高了,沒有意思了。」

20. 「其實,這個問題她的媽媽也跟我聊過,希望我勸勸她。她們雖然知道這個婚姻是假的,但不希望男方知道女方父母知道這個婚姻是假的。就是說,能夠像多了半個兒子那樣,好好的和睦地生活,假裝不知道這個事情,或者是扮演這樣的一個角色,不知道她的事情。如果大家都知道這是假的，她的媽媽會很尷尬，就假裝大家都不知道。」

21. 「他們最多想的就是輿論，和親戚的關係。他們就覺得這個事情妥善地解決掉，問題解決了，你們就出去吧。別人不關注你們了，父母就輕鬆了。」

Chapter 5

1. 「虛假的婚姻，其實是我們對彼此和家庭的承諾。維護著表面的微笑，需要付出的，比任何人能想像的都要多。」

2. Lisa Rofel, *Desiring China: Experiments in Neoliberalism, Sexuality, and Public Culture* (Durham and London: Duke University Press, 2007).

3. For informants born after the 1980s, the implementation of the one-child policy in cities has possibly put many in a further disadvantaged position when dealing with the joint pressure of marriage and childbearing. Yet it is also important to note that the one-child policy has profoundly transformed the relationship between parents and children. While the single-child generation is disadvantaged in some ways—for instance, they have to face the pressure of marriage and childbearing all alone—in other ways, they have more resources in terms of information and personal mobility to cope with the force of sexual conformity. It is an important area for further studies into how changing dynamics between parents and the single-child generation affect the lives of lesbians and gay men in China.

4. 「而中國正好文化很像很中庸的，畢竟它是以父系社會為主的國家，大家沒有明顯的感覺到這種女同志或男同志對社會的衝擊力，大家都是非常的很平穩的在生活。很多男同女同不管怎麼樣到了該結婚的年紀還去結婚了，他的痛苦他的絕望或他的怎麼樣都是在背後陰暗的角落裡的，沒有被那個拿到陽光下面來的，大家覺得看不見就是不存在的，所以也沒有人會過多去關注這個事情，只是很緩慢的偶爾可能會有冰山一角會露出來，說哪裡什麼酒吧同志的色情活動被衝擊啦，或者某兩個人特別的海枯石爛一定要去結婚啊這樣子，這只是作為新聞去報道，還不是那種經常會發生到我們身邊的事情。我覺得基本上還是很寬鬆的，只要你自己能夠調整好自己的心態，就是找到你今後想要找到的道路的話，問題不是很大，沒有到一種就是在國外有時候會擔心人身安全這種地步。」

5. 「同性愛者普遍希望與自己傾心並傾心於自己的人一同生活，但由於社會文明的相對落後，大量同性愛者在歧視的壓力下過著多性伴生活，難以建立良好、穩定、可靠的單一伴侶關係和尋找適合作伴侶的人，他們之中很多人無可奈何地只能與陌生同性發生性關係，以滿足自己的生理需要和深層次心理渴求。這一現狀使他們生活在極易被愛滋病毒和性病感染的高危因素。因此，在愛滋時代，改變歧視同性愛人群的社會環境，是相關學術界重大的義不容辭的責任和義務。」

6. 「另一方面則需要大力普及有關性取向的解放；北歐國家如丹麥，則是通過同性戀社團與學術界溝通，學術界再與政府溝通，政府再教育大眾的方式解決同性戀問題。中國目前走的是北歐的路子，因為這更適合中國國情。與政府保持良性合作關係，團結所有的人，包括不同觀點和態度的人，才能比較好地解決中國同性戀問題。取向的科學知識，使大眾理解、接納同性戀者，消除歧視，進而為同性戀者的良好交流創造空間。」

7. 「在黑夜之後，握著你的手，在陽光下驕傲地走，坦然happy地過我們的生活！」

8. 「中國同性戀人群中，有很多具有現代文化素質，追求著高質量的生活和努力體現生命的價值。一些『活得不錯』的同性戀朋友，都是首先以自己在社會上勤奮上進、有所成功，對父母家人作出貢獻後，終於有勇氣說明自己的性取向。有同性戀者認

為：『同性戀』的含義首先是作為人、擁有人的尊嚴；就尊嚴來說，與是否是同性戀
沒有任何關係。

　　還有同性戀者說：作為同性戀者，我首先提倡行為自律。只有在行為自律的前
提下，才有資格向社會和政府提出寬容和善待的問題。如果沒有行為自律的前提，
一切無從談起。一個國家、群體、公民都應有自律的行為規範，否則很難得到大眾
的認同。做為尚未得到大眾認同的同性戀者來說，更應該注意自身形象問題，樹立
一個高尚、健康、向上的良好社會形象尤為重要。儘管有些規範不一定每個人都能
做得很好，但我們可以努力去做。我們首先應該承擔起社會賦予的角色：遵紀守
法，陶冶高尚的情操，行為自律。只有對自己負責，才可能對別人負責、對社會負
責，才能得到大眾社會的認同。」

9. 「就是說不可能去這樣說你這樣是沒有錯的，完全正確的，你想怎麼樣就怎麼樣。而
是就事論事，而且如果她自我介紹她還在上學的話，我們會告訴她最好把學上好一
點，因為這個不是跟性取向的關係了，是人生很重要的一件事情，你自己都不能自
己做好的話，不可能可以為別人帶來幸福。〔就是說唸完書再講？〕你可以在唸書的
時候談朋友，但是你不能為了這個而放棄一切，你自己都沒有辦法認同自己，把自
己的生活變得好一點，你不能帶給別人任何的安全感，和幸福感。」

10. John Cho (2009) observes that contract marriage in South Korea is uniquely a
middle or upper-middle-class phenomenon. The number of informants I have in
China who are in cooperative marriages is too small to reach any generalization of
class background at the present moment.

Bibliography

In Chinese

Aibai Culture and Education Center. 2006. *Frequently Asked Legal Questions Facing Gays and Lesbians (2nd Edition)* (同志法律常見問題解答(第二版)).

An Keqiang. 1997 (1st edition 1995). *Black Souls under the Red Sun: A Live Report of Mainland Chinese Tongzhi* (紅太陽下的黑靈魂：中國大陸同志現場報導). Taipei: Reai chubanshiye youxiangongsi.

Center for the Study of Sexualities. 1998. *Special Issue: Queer Politics and Queer Theory* (酷兒理論與政治專號), *Working Papers in Gender/ Sexuality Studies*, Nos. 3 and 4. Taiwan: The Center for the Study of Sexualities, Department of English, National Central University.

Chen Guanren and Yi Yang. 2004. *An Investigation of Middle Class in China: An Authoritative Report of Middle Class in China.* (中國中產者調查：來自中國社會中產層的權威報告). Beijing: Tuanjie chubanshe.

Chen Yan. 1999. *Internet Changes China* (Internet 改變中國). Beijing: Beijingdaxue chubanshe.

Chen Yingfang, ed. 2003. *Migrating to Shanghai: An Oral Record of 52 People* (移民上海：52 人的口述實錄). Shanghai: Xuelin chubanshe.

Chen Zhongyi. 2005. *An Unusual Transformation in Chinese Marriage and Family* (中國婚姻家庭非常裂變). Beijing: Zhongyangbianyi chubanshe.

Chou Wah Shan. 1996. *Beijing Tongzhi Stories* (北京同志故事). Hong Kong: Xianggang tongzhiyanjiushe.

Chou Wah Shan. 1997. *Postcolonial Tongzhi* (後殖民同志). Hong Kong: Xianggang tongzhiyanjiushe.

Chou Wah Shan. 2000. *Gender Transgression in China* (性別越界在中國). Hong Kong: Xianggang tongzhiyanjiushe.

Chou Wah Shan, Anson Mak, and Jiang Jianbang, ed. 1995. *Hong Kong Tongzhi Coming Out* (香港同志站出來). Hong Kong: Xianggang tongzhiyanjiushe.

Department of Population and Employment Statistics, the National Bureau of Statistics of China. 2005. *2004 China Population* (中國人口). Beijing: China Statistics Press.

Fang Gang. 1995. *Homosexuality in China* (同性戀在中國). Changchun: Jilinrenmin chubanshe.

Fang Gang. 2005a. *Case Studies of Multiple Sex Partners in China* (中國多性夥伴個案考察). Beijing: Zhongguoshehui chubanshe.

Fang Gang. 2005b. *Sexuality and Gender during the Social Transform in Mainland China Today* (轉型期中國的性與性別). Hong Kong: Xianggangdadao chubanshe.

Fu Guangmin, ed. 2005. *Psychological Map of Women* (女性的心靈地圖). Beijing: Xinshijie chubanshe.

Guo Xiaofei. 2007. *Homosexuality under Chinese Law* (中國法視野下的同性戀). Beijing: Intellectual Property Publishing House.

Hailan. 2005. *My Angel My Love* (我的天使我的愛). Beijing: Zhongguoxiju chubanshe.

He Xiaopei. 2008. "The Past and Present of Female Homosexuals" (女同性戀者的過去與 今天). In Shanghai Nvai Lesbian Group, *Talking about Their Love: An Oral History of Women Who Love Women in Shanghai I* (她們的愛在說：愛上女人的女人・上海・口 述歷史（一）). Shanghai: Shanghai Nvai Lesbian Group.

Jia Ping. 2005. *Report of Rights, Legal Problems and Related Issues of Homosexual (Bisexual) in China* (同（雙）性戀相關法律問題綜述). Beijing: Aizhixing Institute of Health Education.

Jiatingzazhishe jiatingyanjiuzhongxin, ed. 2001. *Chinese Marriage and Family: Development and Vision* (中國婚姻家庭：歷程・前瞻). Beijing: Zhongguofunü chubanshe.

Kam, Y. L. Lucetta. 2011. "A Smile on the Surface: Family Politics of Lalas in Shanghai" (表面的微笑：上海拉拉的家庭政治). In Ding Naifei and Liu Jen-peng (ed.), *Querying the Marriage and Family Continuum* (置疑婚姻家庭連續體). Taipei: Shenlou Press.

Lambda. 1995. *We Are Female Homosexuals* (我們是女同性戀). Taipei: Shuoren chubanshe.

Li Peilin, Li Qiang and Sun Liping. 2004. *Social Stratification in China's Today* (中國社會分 層). Beijing: Social Sciences Documentation Publishing House.

Li Xiaojiang, ed. 1997. *Women Studies Movement: Case Study of China* (婦女研究運動：中國 個案). Hong Kong: Oxford University Press.

Li Xiaojiang et al. 2000. *Women? Feminism?* (女性？主義？). Nanjing: Jiangsurenmin chubanshe.

Li Xiaojiang. 2005. *Academic Questions on Women/ Gender* (女性／性別的學術問題). Jinan: Shandongrenmin chubanshe.

Li Yinhe. 1999. *On Sexuality* (性的問題). Beijing: Zhongguoqingnian chubanshe.

Li Yinhe. 2002a. *Subculture of Homosexuality* (同性戀亞文化). Beijing: Zhongguoyouyi chubanshe.

Li Yinhe. 2002b. *Love and Sexuality of the Chinese Women* (中國女性的感情與性). Beijing: Zhongguoyouyi chubanshe.

Li Yinhe. 2002c. *Love, Sexuality, and Marriage of the Chinese People* (中國人的性愛與婚姻). Beijing: Zhongguoyouyi chubanshe.

Li Yinhe. 2003a. *Sexual Culture Research* (性文化研究報告). Nanjing: Jiangsurenmin chubanshe.

Li Yinhe. 2003b. *The Rise of Women's Power* (女性權力的崛起). Beijing: Wenhuayishu chubanshe.

Li Yinhe. 2005. *You Need to be Comforted So Much* (你如此需要安慰). Beijing: Dangdaishijie chubanshe.

Li Yinhe, and Wang Xiaobo. 1992. *Their World: Looking into the Male Homosexual Group in China* (他們的世界：中國男同性戀群落透視). Hong Kong: Cosmos Books.

Liu Baoju. 2006. *Family in a Changing Society: A Study of Contemporary Urban Family in China* (社會變遷中的家庭：當代中國城市家庭研究). Chengdu: Sichuanchubanjituan bashu shushe.

Liu Dalin, ed. 1992. *Sexual Behaviour in Modern China: A Report of the Nation-wide "Sex Civilization" Survey on 20,000 Subjects in China* (中國當代性文化：中國兩萬例 "性文明" 調查報告). Shanghai: Shenghuo, dushu, xinzhi sanlianshudian shanghaifendian.

Liu Dalin et al. 1998. *Sociologist Perspective: The Transformation of Marriage and Family in China* (社會學家的觀點：中國婚姻家庭變遷). Beijing: Zhongguoshehui chubanshe.

Liu Dalin. 2000. *Sexual Behaviour in Twentieth Century China* (20世紀中國性文化). Shanghai: Shanghaisanlian chubanshe.

Liu Dalin, and Lu Longguang, ed. 2004. *Study of Homosexuality in China* (中國同性戀研究). Beijing: Zhongguoshehui chubanshe.

Liu Huaqin. 2005. *Tianya Virtual Community: Text-Based Social Interactions on the Internet* (天涯虛擬社區：互聯網上基於文本的社會互動研究). Beijing: Minzu chubanshe.

Liu Renpeng, Ding Naifei and Amie Elizabeth Parry. 2007. *Penumbrae Query Shadow: Queer Reading Tactics* (含蓄美學與酷兒政略). Taoyuan, Taiwan: NCU Sex/Gender Studies Center.

Lu Xueyi, ed. 2004. *Social Mobility in Contemporary China* (當代中國社會流動). Beijing: Social Sciences Documentation Publishing House.

Lu Yilong. 2004. *Transgressing Hukou: Understanding the Household Registration System in China* (超越戶口——解讀中國戶籍制度). Beijing: Zhongguoshehuikexue chubanshe.

Ma Ping. 2011. *Homosexual Issues from the Perspective of Constitutional Law* (同性戀問題的憲法學思考). Beijing: Law Press China.

Ma Xiaohua. 2003. *The Study of Sex* (性的學習). Beijing: Zhongguorenkou chubanshe.

Ma Xiaonian, and Yang Dazhong. 2005. *Report of an Internet Sexual Health Survey of Chinese Women* (中國女性性調查報告). Beijing: Guangmingribao chubanshe.

Maizuideyangui. 2007. *Why I Love You So Much* (那麼愛妳為什麼). Taipei: Beijizhiguang chubanyouxiangongsi.

Martin, Fran. 1998. "Closet, Mask, Membrane: The Logic of Yin/Xian of Tongzhi Subjectivities in Contemporary Taiwan Discourses" (衣櫃、面具、膜：當代台灣論述中同性主體的隱／現邏輯). *Chung-Wai Literary Monthly*, 26(12), pp. 130–149.

Martin, Fran. 2003. "The Crocodile Unmasked: Towards a Theory of *Xianshen*" (揭下面具的鱷魚：邁向一個現身的理論). *Journal of Women's and Gender Studies*, Issue 15, May 2003, pp. 1–36.

Oriental Morning Post. Year missing, circa 2000. *Shanghai Middle Class Landscape* (上海中產全景報告). Shanghai: Shanghai shehuikexue chubanshe.

Pan Suiming. 1995. *Current Sexual Condition in China* (中國性現狀). Beijing: Guangmingribao chubanshe.

Pan Suiming, ed. 2004. *Sexual Lives in the Age of AIDS* (艾滋病時代的性生活). Guangzhou: Nanfangribao chubanshe.

Pan Suiming, ed. 2005. *Discussion and Construction of the Concept of "Xing": The Elements and Mission of Sexuality Research in Contemporary China* (中國 "性" 研究的起點與使命). Kaohsiung, Taiwan: Wanyou chubanshe.

Pan Suiming, William Parish, Wang Aili and Edward Lauman. 2004. *Sexual Behavior and Relation in Contemporary China* (當代中國人的性行為與性關係). Beijing: Social Sciences Academic Press (China).

Pan Suiming, and Yang Rui. 2004. *Sexuality of Chinese College Students: A Ten-Year Longitude Nationwide Random Study* (性愛十年：全國大學生性行為的追蹤調查). Beijing: Social Sciences Academic Press (China).

Pan Suiming, and Zeng Jing. 2000. *Sexual Attitude and Behaviour of Contemporary Chinese College Students* (中國當代大學生的性觀念與性行為). Beijing: Commercial Press.

Pan Suiming et al. 2008. *The Accomplishment of Sexuality Revolution in China: Preliminary Reports on a Compared Study Between 2000 and 2006* (中國性革命成功的實證：全國成年人口隨機抽樣調查結果簡報2000年與2006年的對照研究). Kaohsiung, Taiwan: Wanyou chubanshe.

Rong Weiyi. 2002. "Mapping Homosexuality Study in Contemporary China" (盤點當代中國同性戀研究). *Friend Exchange* (朋友通信), pp. 33–49.

Ruan Fangfu. 1989. "Homosexuality: An Unresolved Puzzle" (同性戀———個未解之謎). In *Sexuality and Medicine* (性學與醫學). Hong Kong: Jinling chubanshe.

Shanghai Nvai Lesbian Group. 2008. *Talking about Their Love: An Oral History of Women Who Love Women in Shanghai I* (她們的愛在說：愛上女人的女人‧上海‧口述歷史（一）). Shanghai: Shanghai Nvai Lesbian Group.

Shen Chonglin, and Yang Shanhua, ed. 1995. *Family Study in Contemporary Cities in China* (當代中國城市家庭研究). Beijing: Zhongguoshehuikexue chubanshe.

Shen Hao, ed. 2005. *Talking Sex and Love* (談什麼性說什麼愛). Shanghai: Wenhui chubanshe.

Sun Zhongxin, James Farrer and Kyung-hee Choi. 2005. "Sexual Identity among Men Who Have Sex with Men in Shanghai." In *Discussion and Construction of the Concept "Xing": The Elements and Mission of Sexuality Research in Contemporary China* (中國 "性" 研究的起點與使命). Kaohsiung: Wanyou chubanshe.

Taiwan Tongzhi Hotline Association, ed. 2003. *Parents of Lesbians and Gays Talk about Their Experiences* (親愛的爸媽，我是同志). Taipei: PsyGarden Publishing Company.

Wang Chao. 2007. *Falling Flowers and Flowing Stream* (花自飄落水自流). Beijing: Huaxia chubanshe.

Wu Chunsheng, and Chou Wah Shan, ed. 1996. *We Are Alive* (我們活著). Hong Kong: Xianggangtongzhi yanjiushe.

Yi Zhaoying, ed. 2005. *Social Transformation and Intellectual Women in Cities: A Study of Colleges in Shanghai* (社會轉型與都市知識女性：來自上海高校的研究報告). Beijing: Zhongguoshehuikexue chubanshe.

Zeng Baoying. 2000. *Study on the Process of Interaction Between Homosexual Subjects and Family* (Master Thesis) (同性戀主體與家庭關係互動歷程探索). Taiwan: Department of Applied Psychology, Fu-Jen Catholic University.

Zhang Beichuan. 1994. *Homosexuality* (同性愛). Shandongkexuejishu chubanshe.

Zhang Juanfen. 1998. *Against the Wall* (姊妹戲牆：女同志運動學). Taipei: UNITAS Publishing Co.

Zhang Juanfen. 2001. *Lesbians Like This and That* (愛的自由式——女同志故事書). Taipei: China Times Publishing Company.

Zhang Mingyuan. 1981. "Phenomenon of Homosexuality in the Red Chamber" (《紅樓》中的同性戀現象). In *Popular Medicine* (大眾醫學), Issue 3, February, pp. 42–46.

Zhao Yanning. 2001. "Mask and Reality: The Problem of 'Xianshen' in Taiwan Tongzhi Movement" (面具與真實:論台灣同志運動的「現身」問題). In *Travelling with a Grass Hat: Sex/Gender, Power, Nation* (戴著草帽到處旅行:性/別、權力、國家). Taipei: Chuliu Publisher.

Zheng Hangsheng, and Li Lulu. 2004. *Social Structure of the Cities in Contemporary China* (當代中國城市社會結構:現狀與趨勢). Beijing: Zhongguo renmindaxue chubanshe.

Zheng Meili. 1997. *Women's Circle: Gender, Family and Community Life of Female Tongzhis in Taiwan* (女兒圈:台灣女同志的性別、家庭與圈內生活). Taipei: Fem Books.

Zhou Dan, ed. 2006. *Homosexuality and Law: Articles and Information of the "International Conference on Sexuality, Policies and Law"* (同性戀與法:"性、政策與法國際學術研討會"論文及資料). Guilin, China: Guangxi Normal University Press.

Zhou Dan. 2009. *Desires and Discipline: Legal Interpretations of Same-sex Desires in Chinese Modernity* (愛悅與規訓:中國現代性中同性慾望的法理現象). Guilin, China: Guangxi Normal University Press.

Zhou Xiaohung, ed. 2005. *Survey of the Chinese Middle Class* (中國中產階層調查). Beijing: Social Sciences Academic Press (China).

In English

Acker, Sandra. 2000. "In/Out/Side: Positioning the Researcher in Feminist Qualitative Research", *Resources for Feminist Research*, Issue 28 (1/2), pp. 189–208.

Ainley, Rosa, ed. 1998. *New Frontiers of Space, Bodies and Gender*. London and New York: Routledge.

Bell, David, and Gill Valentine, ed. 1995. *Mapping Desire*. London and New York: Routledge.

Bell, David, and Gill Valentine. 1995. "The Sexed Self: Strategies of Performance, Sites of Resistance." In Steven Pile and Nigel Thrift (ed.), *Mapping the Subject: Geographies of Cultural Transformation*. London and New York: Routledge.

Benhabib, Seyla. 1998. "Models of Public Space: Hannah Arendt, the Liberal Tradition, and Jurgen Habermas." In Joan B. Landes (ed.), *Feminism, the Public and the Private*. Oxford, New York: Oxford University Press.

Bernstein, Mary, and Renate Reimann, ed. 2001. *Queer Families, Queer Politics*. New York: Columbia University Press.

Berry, Chris. 2001. "Asian Values, Family Values: Film, Video, and Lesbian and Gay Identities." In Gerard Sullivan and Peter A. Jackson (ed.) *Gay and Lesbian Asia: Culture, Identity, Community*. New York, London, Oxford: Harrington Park Press.

Berry, Chris, Fran Martin, and Audrey Yue, ed. 2003. *Mobile Cultures: New Media in Queer Asia*. Durham and London: Duke University Press.

Brown, Wendy. 2006. *Regulating Aversion: Tolerance in the Age of Identity and Empire*. Princeton and Oxford: Princeton University Press.

Brownell, Susan, and Jeffery N. Wasserstrom. 2002. *Chinese Femininities Chinese Masculinities: A Reader*. Berkeley: University of California Press.

Calhoun, Cheshire. 2000. *Feminism, the Family, and the Politics of the Closet*. Oxford, New York: Oxford University Press.

Calhoun, Craig, ed. 1992. *Habermas and the Public Sphere*. Cambridge, MA: MIT Press.

Case, Sue-Ellen. 1998. "Making Butch: An Historical Memoir of the 1970s." In Sally R. Munt (ed.), *Butch/ Femme: Inside Lesbian Gender*. London: Cassell.

Castells, Manuel. 1989. *The Informational City: Information Technology, Economic Restructuring, and the Urban-Regional Process*. Oxford: B. Blackwell.

Chen, Yaya, and Yiqing Chen. 2006. "Lesbians in China's Mainland: A Brief Introduction." In Saori Kamano and Diana Khor (eds.), "'Lesbians' in East Asia: Diversity, Identities, and Resistance," *Journal of Lesbian Studies*, Vol. 10, Nos. 3/4, pp. 113–125.

Cho, John (Song Pae). 2009. "The Wedding Banquet Revisited: 'Contract Marriages' between Korean Gays and Lesbians." *Anthropology Quarterly*, Volume 8, Number 2, pp. 401–422.

Clark, Diane. 1993. "Commodity Lesbianism." In Henry Abelove, Michele Aina Barale, and David M. Halperin (ed.), *The Lesbian and Gay Studies Reader*. New York: Routledge.

Cohen, Jean L. 1995. "Critical Social Theory and Feminist Critiques: The Debate with Jurgen Habermas." In Johanna Meeham (ed.), *Feminists Read Habermas: Gendering the Subject of Discourse*. New York and London: Routledge.

Duggan, Lisa. 2003. *The Twilight of Equality? Neoliberalism, Cultural Politics, and the Attack On Democracy*. Boston: Beacon Press.

Duncan, Nancy. 1996. "Renegotiating Gender and Sexuality in Public and Private Spaces." In Nancy Duncan (ed.), *Bodyspace: Destabilizing Geographies of Gender and Sexuality*. London and New York: Routledge.

Eley, Geoff. 1992. "Nations, Publics, and Political Cultures: Placing Habermas in the Nineteenth Century." In Craig Calhoun (ed.), *Habermas and the Public Sphere*. Cambridge, MA: MIT Press.

Eng, David L. 2010. "The Queer Space of China: Expressive Desire in Stanley Kwan's *Lan Yu*." *Positions*, Vol. 18, No. 2, pp. 459–487.

Engebretsen, Elisabeth Lund. 2009. "Intimate Practices, Conjugal Ideals: Affective Ties and Relationship Strategies Among Lala (Lesbian) Women in Contemporary Beijing." *Sexuality Research & Social Policy: Journal of NSRC*, 6(3), pp. 3–14.

Evans, Harriet. 1997. *Women and Sexuality in China: Female Sexuality and Gender Since 1949*. New York: The Continuum Publishing Company.

Farrer, James. 2002. *Opening Up: Youth Sex Culture and Market Reform in Shanghai*. Chicago and London: The University of Chicago Press.

Fleming, Marie. 1995. "Women and the 'Public Use of Reason'." In Johanna Meeham (ed.), *Feminists Read Habermas: Gendering the Subject of Discourse*. New York and London: Routledge.

Fraser, Nancy. 1990. "Rethinking the Public Sphere: A Contribution to the Critique of Actually Existing Democracy." *Social Text*, No. 25/26, pp. 56–80.

Fraser, Nancy. 1995. "What's Critical about Critical Theory?" In Johanna Meeham (ed.), *Feminists Read Habermas: Gendering the Subject of Discourse*. New York and London: Routledge.

Giddens, Anthony. 1990. *The Consequences of Modernity*. Stanford, CA: Stanford University Press.

Grosz, Elizabeth. 1994. *Volatile Bodies: Toward a Corporeal Feminism*. Bloomington and Indianapolis: Indiana University Press.

Halberstam, Judith. 2005. *In a Queer Time and Space: Transgender Bodies, Subcultural Lives*. New York: New York University Press.

Harding, Sandra. 1986. "The Social Construction of Human Sexuality." In *The Science Question in Feminism*. Milton Keynes, England: Open University Press.

Harvey, David. 1989. *The Urban Experience*. Baltimore: Johns Hopkins University Press.

He Xiaopei. 2002. "Chinese Women *Tongzhi* Organizing in the 1990s." *Inter-Asia Cultural Studies*, Volume 3, Number 3, 2002, pp. 479–491.

He Xiaopei. 2010. "My Unconventional Marriage or ménage à trois in Beijing." In Yau Ching (ed.), *As Normal As Possible: Negotiating Sexuality and Gender in Mainland China and Hong Kong*. Hong Kong: Hong Kong University Press.

Ho, Loretta Wing Wah. 2010. *Gay and Lesbian Subculture in Urban China*. London and New York: Routledge.

Hughes, Christopher R., and Gudrun Wacker, ed. 2003. *China and the Internet: Politics of the Digital Leap Forward*. London and New York: RoutledgeCurzon.

Ingram, Gordon Brent, Anne-Marie Bouthillette, and Yolanda Retter, ed. 1997. *Queers in Space: Communities, Public Places, Sites of Resistance*. Washington: Bay Press.

Jackson A. Peter. 2001. "Pre-Gay, Post-Queer: Thai Perspectives on Proliferating Gender/Sex Diversity in Asia." In Gerard Sullivan and Peter A. Jackson (ed.), *Gay and Lesbian Asia: Culture, Identity, Community*. New York, London, Oxford: Harrington Park Press.

Jeffreys, Elaine, ed. 2006. *Sex and Sexuality in China*. London and New York: Routledge.

Kam, Y. L. Lucetta. 2006. "Noras on the Road: Family and Marriage of Lesbian Women in Shanghai." In Saori Kamano and Diana Khor (eds.), "'Lesbians' in East Asia: Diversity, Identities, and Resistance", *Journal of Lesbian Studies*, Vol. 10, Nos. 3/4, pp. 87–103.

Kam, Y. L. Lucetta. 2010. "Opening Up Marriage: Married Lalas in Shanghai." In Yau Ching (ed.), *As Normal As Possible: Negotiating Sexuality and Gender in Mainland China and Hong Kong*. Hong Kong: Hong Kong University Press.

Kang Wenqing. 2009. *Obsession: Male Same-sex Relations in China, 1900–1950*. Hong Kong: Hong Kong University Press.

Karl, Irmi. 2007. "On-/Offline: Gender, Sexuality, and the Techno-Politics of Everyday Life." In Kate O'Riordan and David J. Philips (ed.), *Queer Online: Media, Technology and Sexuality*. New York: Peter Lang Publishing, Inc.

Kluver, Randy and Jack Linchuan Qiu. 2003. "China, the Internet and Democracy." In Indrajit Banerjee (ed.), *Rhetoric and Reality: The Internet Challenge for Democracy in Asia*. Singapore: Eastern Universities Press.

Kong, S. K. Travis. 2010. "Outcast Bodies: Money, Sex and Desire of Money Boys in Mainland China." In Yau Ching (ed.), *As Normal As Possible: Negotiating Sexuality and Gender in Mainland China and Hong Kong*. Hong Kong: Hong Kong University Press.

Kong, S. K. Travis. 2011. *Chinese Male Homosexualities: Memba, Tongzhi and Golden Boy*. London and New York: Routledge.

Landes, Joan B. 1995. "The Public and the Private Sphere: A Feminist Reconsideration." In Johanna Meeham (ed.), *Feminists Read Habermas: Gendering the Subject of Discourse*. New York and London: Routledge.

Landes, Joan B., ed. 1998. *Feminism, the Public and the Private*. Oxford, New York: Oxford University Press.

Laukkanen, Marjo. 2007. "Young Queers Online: The Limits and Possibilities of Non-Heterosexual Self-Representation in Online Conversations." In Kate O'Riordan and David J. Philips (ed.), *Queer Online: Media, Technology and Sexuality.* New York: Peter Lang Publishing, Inc.

Li Yinghe. 2006. "Regulating Male Same-Sex Relationships in the People's Republic of China." In Elaine Jeffreys (ed.), *Sex and Sexuality in China.* London and New York: Routledge.

Liu Jen-peng, and Ding Naifei. 2005. "Reticent Poetics, Queer Politics." *Inter-Asia Cultural Studies,* Volume 6, Number 1, pp. 30–55.

Mansfield, Nick. 2000. *Subjectivity: Theories of the Self from Freud to Haraway.* New York: New York University Press.

Martin, Fran. 2000a. "From Citizenship to Queer Counterpublic: Reading Taipei's New Park." *Communal/ Plural,* Vol. 8, No. 1, 2000, pp. 81–94.

Martin, Fran. 2000b. "Surface Tensions: Reading Productions of *Tongzhi* in Contemporary Taiwan." *GLQ,* 6(1), pp. 61–86.

McMillan, Joanna. 2006. *Sex, Science and Morality in China.* London and New York: Routledge.

Medhurst, Andy, and Sally R. Munt, ed. 1997. *Lesbian and Gay Studies: A Critical Introduction.* London and Washington: Cassell.

Munt, Sally R. 1998. *Heroic Desire: Lesbian Identity and Cultural Space.* New York: New York University Press.

O'Riordan, Kate. 2007. "Queer Theories and Cybersubjects: Intersecting Figures." In Kate O'Riordan and David J. Philips (ed.), *Queer Online: Media, Technology and Sexuality.* New York: Peter Lang Publishing, Inc.

Ortner, Sherry B. 1998. "Is Female to Male as Nature Is to Culture?" In Joan B. Landes (ed.), *Feminism, the Public and the Private.* Oxford, New York: Oxford University Press.

Pate, Carol. 1989. "Feminist Critiques of the Public/Private Dichotomy." In *The Disorder of Women: Democracy, Feminism, and Political Theory.* Stanford, CA: Stanford University Press.

Plummer, Ken, ed. 2002. *Sexualities: Critical Concepts in Sociology (Volume II).* London and New York: Routledge.

Plummer, Ken. 2003. *Intimate Citizenship: Private Decisions and Public Dialogues.* Montreal and Kingston: McGill-Queen's University Press.

Probyn, Elspeth. 1995. "Lesbians in Space: Gender, Sex and the Structure of Missing." *Gender, Place and Culture,* 2(1), pp. 77–84.

Ryan, Mary P. 1992, "Gender and Public Access: Women's Politics in Nineteenth-Century America." In Craig Calhoun (ed.), *Habermas and the Public Sphere.* Cambridge, MA: MIT Press.

Richardson, Diane. 2000. "Part 2: Sexual Citizenship." In *Rethinking Sexuality.* London, Thousand Oaks, New Delhi: Sage Publications.

Richardson, Diane, and Steven Seidman, ed. 2002. *Handbook of Lesbian and Gay Studies.* London, Thousand Oaks and New Delhi: Sage Publications.

Rofel, Lisa. 1999. "Qualities of Desire: Imagining Gay Identities in China." *GLQ,* 5(4), pp. 451–474.

Rofel, Lisa. 2007. *Desiring China: Experiments in Neoliberalism, Sexuality, and Public Culture.* Durham and London: Duke University Press.

Rosaldo, Michelle Zimbalist. 2002. "Woman, Culture, and Society: A Theoretical Overview." In Nancy P. McKee and Linda Stone (ed.), *Readings in Gender and Culture in America.* Stone Upper Saddle River, NJ: Prentice Hall.

Ruan Fangfu. 1991. *Sex in China: Studies in Sexology in Chinese Culture.* New York: Plenum Press.

Sang, Tze-lan D. 2003. *The Emerging Lesbian: Female Same-Sex Desire in Modern China.* Chicago and London: The University of Chicago Press.

Seidman, Steven. 2002. *Beyond the Closet: The Transformation of Gay and Lesbian Life.* New York and London: Routledge.

Shen, James Jinguo. 2002. "Computer-Mediated Communication: Internet Development and New Challenges in China." In Wenshan Jia, Xing Lu, and D. Ray Heisey (ed.), *Chinese Communication Theory and Research: Reflections, New Frontiers, and New Directions.* Westport, CT; London: Alex Publishing.

Stacey, Judith. 1988. "Can There Be a Feminist Ethnography?" *Women's Studies Int. Forum,* Vol. 11, No. 1, pp. 21–27.

Thompson, John B. 1995. *The Media and Modernity: A Social Theory of the Media.* Cambridge: Polity Press.

Valentine, Gill. 1996. "(Re)Negotiating the 'Heterosexual Street': Lesbian Productions of Space." In Nancy Duncan (ed.), *Bodyspace: Destabilizing Geographies of Gender and Sexuality.* London and New York: Routledge.

Valentine, Gill. 1997. "(Hetero)Sexing Space: Lesbian Perceptions and Experiences of Everyday Spaces." In Linda McDowell and Joanne P. Sharp (ed.), *Space, Gender, Knowledge: Feminist Readings.* London: Arnold.

Valentine, Gill. 2002. "Queer Bodies and the Production of Space." In Diane Richardson and Steven Seidman (ed.), *Handbook of Lesbian and Gay Studies.* London, Thousand Oaks and New Delhi: Sage Publications.

Wan, Yanhai. 2001. "Becoming a Gay Activist in Contemporary China." In Gerard Sullivan and Peter A. Jackson (ed.), *Gay and Lesbian Asia: Culture, Identity, Community.* New York, London, Oxford: Harrington Park Press.

Wang, Hui. 2003. *China's New Order: Society, Politics, and Economy in Transition.* Cambridge, MA: Harvard University Press.

Warner, Michael. 1991. "Introduction: Fear of a Queer Planet." *Social Text,* 29, pp. 3–17.

Warner, Michael. 2002. *Publics and Counterpublics.* New York: Zone Books.

Weeks, Jeffrey, Janet Holland and Matthew Waites, ed. 2003. *Sexualities and Society: A Reader.* Cambridge, UK; Malden, MA: Polity Press in association with Blackwell.

Wei, Bu. 2004. "Women and the Internet in China." In Peter H. Smith, Jennifer L. Troutuer, and Christine Hünefeldt (ed.), *Promises of Empowerment: Women in Asia and Latin America.* Lanham, MD: Rowman and Littlefield Publishers, Inc.

Wong, Kit Mui Day. 2004. "(Post-)identity Politics and Anti-Normalization: (Homo) Sexual Rights Movement." In Agnes S. Ku and Ngai Pun (ed.), *Remaking Citizenship in Hong Kong: Community, Nation, and the Global City.* London and New York: Routledge, pp. 195–214.

Woo, Margaret Y. K. 2006. "Contesting Citizenship: Marriage and Divorce in the People's Republic of China." In Elaine Jeffreys (ed.), *Sex and Sexuality in China*. London and New York: Routledge.

Xu Xiaohe. 1998. "The Social Origins of Historical Changes in Freedom of Mate Choice under State Socialism: The Case of Urban China." In Zhang Jie and Li Xiaobing (ed.), *Social Transition in China*. Lanham, New York, Oxford: University Press of America, Inc.

Yang, Mayfair Mei-hui, ed. 1999. *Spaces of Their Own: Women's Public Sphere in Transnational China*. Minneapolis, MN: University of Minnesota Press.

Yau, Ching. 2010. *As Normal As Possible: Negotiating Sexuality and Gender in Mainland China and Hong Kong*. Hong Kong: Hong Kong University Press.

Zhan, Heying Jenny. 1996. "Chinese Femininity and Social Control: Gender-Role Socicialization and the State." *Journal of Historical Sociology*, 9(3), pp. 269–289.

Zhang, Lening, and Deng Xiaogang. 1998. "The Effects of Structural Changes in Community and Work Unit in China." In Zhang Jie and Li Xiaobing (ed.), *Social Transition in China*. Lanham, New York, Oxford: University Press of America, Inc.

Zhao, Yuezhi. 2008. "Reconfiguring Party-State Power: Market Reforms, Communication, and Control in the Digital Age." *Communication in China: Political Economy, Power, and Conflict*. Lanham, MD: Rowman and Littlefield Publishers, Inc.

Zheng, Yongnian. 2008. *Technological Empowerment: The Internet, State, and Society in China*. Stanford, CA: Stanford University Press.

Zhong, Xueping, Wang Zheng, and Bai Di, ed. 2001. *Some of Us: Chinese Women Growing Up in the Mao Era*. New Brunswick, NJ: Rutgers University Press.

Index

Note: Terms in italics indicate names of events, video works, institutions, organizations, commercial spaces, or Chinese *pinyin*.